United States Congress Senate, John Sherman

Interview between the United States Senate Committee

On Finance and the Hon. John Sherman, Secretary of the Treasury, on

Refunding, Resumption, Legal-Tenders for Customs Dues

United States Congress Senate, John Sherman

Interview between the United States Senate Committee
On Finance and the Hon. John Sherman, Secretary of the Treasury, on Refunding,
Resumption, Legal-Tenders for Customs Dues

ISBN/EAN: 9783337163396

Printed in Europe, USA, Canada, Australia, Japan

Cover: Foto ©Suzi / pixelio.de

More available books at **www.hansebooks.com**

INTERVIEW

BETWEEN THE

UNITED STATES SENATE COMMITTEE ON FINANCE

AND THE

HON. JOHN SHERMAN,

SECRETARY OF THE TREASURY,

ON

REFUNDING, RESUMPTION, LEGAL-TENDERS FOR CUSTOMS DUES, SINKING FUND, AND KINDRED SUBJECTS.

JANUARY 30, 1880.

1 SH

UNITED STATES SENATE
COMMITTEE ON FINANCE,
January 30, 1880.

In special session. Present: The chairman, Senators Kernan, Wallace, Beck, Morrill, Allison, Ferry.

Secretary SHERMAN stated that he appeared before the committee in obedience to their request.

The CHAIRMAN of the Committee stated that a number of propositions upon which it was desired to obtain the Secretary's views, had been submitted by Senator Beck, a member of the committee, and then read the same, as follows:

1. What reason, if any, there is for refusing to pass a bill authorizing the receipt of legal-tenders for customs dues.

2. Why the trade dollar should not be converted into a standard dollar.

3. What has been the cost of converting the interest-bearing debt, as it stood July 14th, 1870, to what it is now, including double interest, commissions, traveling expenses of agents, &c., and the use of public money by banks, and the value of its use, so as to determine whether the system should be continued or changed.

4. The effect the abolition of the legal-tender quality of greenbacks upon the paper currency.

5. The necessity for a sinking fund and how it is managed.

6. Whether silver coin received in payment of customs duties has been paid out for interest upon the public debt; and if not, why not.

Senator ALLISON desired to know if this interview was to be stenographically reported, and the committee decided that it should be.

UNITED STATES NOTES FOR CUSTOMS DUES.

The CHAIRMAN. Mr. Secretary, will you address your answer to the first proposition:

"What reason, if any, is there for refusing to pass a bill authorizing the receipt of legal-tenders for customs dues?"

Secretary SHERMAN. The act of February 25, 1862 (section 3694, R. S.), provides that all the duties on imported goods shall be paid in coin; and the coin so paid shall be set apart as a special fund to be applied to two purposes, one of which is the payment in coin of interest on the bonds and notes of the United States.

This is the obligation of the government that its coin revenue should be applied to the payment of interest on the public debt. So long as legal-tender notes are maintained at par and parties are willing to receive them in payment of coin interest, there is no objection to receiving legal-tender notes for customs dues.

Since resumption it has been the practice of the department to thus receive them, but this practice can be kept up only as long as parties holding interest obligations are willing to accept the same notes in payment thereof. If, by any unforeseen and untoward event, the notes should again depreciate in value below coin, the obligations of the government would still require that interest on the public debt be paid in coin; and if customs dues were payable in legal-tender notes, the de-

4

partment would have no source from which to obtaiu the coin necessary to the payment of interest, for of course holders of interest obligations would not accept a depreciated currency when they were entitled by law to coin. In addition, I would add that in my annual report of December, 1878 (a year ago), I stated to Congress, after a pretty full examination, I thought it was my duty to give notice that on the 1st of January I would receive United States notes for customs duties, therein giving pretty full reasons for doing it, and I hoped then that Congress would take some action about it; but I have come to the conclusion since that it had better be allowed to stand just as it is—that as long as both parties, the government and the citizen, are willing to receive and take United States notes we had better let them do so, leaving the government the right to demand payment in coin for customs duties and the individual the authority to demand coin for interest of public debt.

The CHAIRMAN. My objection is, that it disposes of the contract between the government and the holder of its obligations—which is, in my view, a fixed contract only to be rescinded by mutual consent, and substitutes a mere order of the Treasury Department. I admit that practically it is enough that as long as the notes are equal to coin you may receive them; but the very moment the legal tenders depreciate there is a substantial as well as technical violation of the contract. My feeling is, and I have so argued in the Senate and elsewhere, that the law is quite enough as it stands; and though you made the very person who received these duties the redeeming agent of the government notes, I do not think still that the customs duties can be lawfully receivable in anything else than that which the law requires.

Mr. ALLISON. What would be the objection to a provision substantially of this character: Say that, " as long as the Treasury notes are convertible into coin at the sub-treasury in New York."

The CHAIRMAN. " Redeemable" is the word.

Mr. ALLISON. Well, convertible into or redeemable in coin, they shall be received for customs dues.

Secretary SHERMAN. I have no objection at all to that. This order was made simply to avoid the inconvenience to the individual of presenting his notes at the sub-treasury, then carrying the coin received there to the custom-house, and then compelling the custom-house officer to take it back to the sub-treasury for deposit.

The CHAIRMAN. Of course it was like an idle form, but it was an honest one.

Mr. ALLISON. That would continue our obligation, and, at the same time, relieve you from what some now object to as a technical violation of a statute.

Secretary SHERMAN. I will say that I issued this order with great reluctance, only after full examination, and upon the statement of the Attorney-General, who thought technically I could treat the note as a coin-certificate.

The CHAIRMAN. It might be that practically in its result.

Secretary SHERMAN. We have always received coin certificates in payment of customs dues.

Mr. FERRY. Then, if the law should require you to receive these notes in payment of customs dues, what would be the objection, as long as they are redeemable in coin, for you are required by law to redeem them in coin, and that would be merely a method of redemption and it would not matter whether you had actually redeemed them and paid out the coin or received them in payment for duties. Would not the declaration that they should be received in payment of customs dues as long as they are redeemable in coin cover the ground ?

Mr. ALLISON. Not as long as redeemable, but as long as redeemed in coin.

Mr. FERRY. Then, that would imply that the government could reach a point in its fiscal condition where it would not redeem in coin.

Secretary SHERMAN. I assumed that the United States would redeem in coin, and that this note was in effect a coin-certificate that so much coin was in the Treasury awaiting demand. It seemed a great inconvenience to compel actual redemption of notes and actual payment of customs dues in coin, and a great popular outcry was being made on that account. I thought, therefore, I would make that order to receive the notes for customs dues, leaving it to Congress, (this order having been made during its session), to check me if I was assuming undue power.

The CHAIRMAN. It was but technical, because you could by law pay these notes in coin or in a coin-certificate, and that coin-certificate is coin. It was simply a question of certifying that the coin was there subject to demand. But it is proposed now by a law to repeal the act of 1862.

Mr. WALLACE. The apprehension in regard to this subject-matter is that there may come a period when United States notes cannot be redeemed in coin, that such a contingency may arise.

Secretary SHERMAN. O, certainly; it may arise under any form of paper money that has ever been devised.

Mr. WALLACE. Are you not to-day in a position in which you can at all hazards keep the United States notes redeemable in coin ?

Secretary SHERMAN. I cannot foresee any condition of circumstances likely to arise in which the United States cannot redeem its notes in coin. We have $148,000,000 of coin in reserve over and above all liabilities; but still we know that wars may come, pestilence may come, an adverse balance of trade, or some contingency of a kind which we cannot know of in advance may arise. I therefore think it is wise to save the right of the United States to demand coin for customs duties if it should be driven to that exigency.

Mr. WALLACE. That is a remote contingency.

The CHAIRMAN. Do you not think it is the right of the creditor ?

Secretary SHERMAN. It is only possible through the consent of the creditor, for when the creditor demands coin we never pay him notes.

The CHAIRMAN. I was speaking in regard to the payment of these duties in coin ; do you regard that as a right the creditor can demand ?

Secretary SHERMAN. It is a right that he would not care to ask for. It is for his convenience that customs dues are paid in notes.

Mr. WALLACE. Suppose you made United States notes convertible into coin at every United States depository and receivable for all forms of government indebtedness—would not that be a practical means of keeping them at par, and maintaining always their equality with coin ?

Secretary SHERMAN. There is one part of your proposition that I would not advocate. I do not think it would be wise to make the government notes redeemable anywhere except in one place—that place being such one as Congress may direct. The experience of other nations has proved that there must be one central reservoir where all demands must be met.

Mr. WALLACE. Should not the government notes be receivable, and interchangeable at every government depository?

Secretary SHERMAN. They should all be received everywhere at par with coin; but whether we should pay coin on obligations except at one place is a matter which I have doubt in regard to.

Mr. WALLACE. What has been the practice of the government in that regard?

The CHAIRMAN. It never had anything to redeem except the greenbacks.

Secretary SHERMAN. Exchange on New York is generally at par or a premium, and practically we so act. We do pay in gold wherever anybody wants it ordinarily, but we usually pay by drafts on New York, and they can be collected without loss to the holders.

Mr. FERRY. I would like to ask if, in your judgment, the receivability of greenbacks for customs dues would not tend to keep the value of the notes equal to gold?

Secretary SHERMAN. I think so.

Mr. FERRY. If that be the case, the law of 1862 having been passed when our credit was low, and we had substantially no gold in the Treasury, and our present credit being high, with a large surplus of gold ample to redeem all notes outstanding, ought we now as a great government, in a time of peace and prosperity shield ourselves under a statute passed in our straits of 1862? Would it not be fairer for a government in our present condition to take its paper that it considers equal to coin for duties, and thus make it equal to coin.

Secretary SHERMAN. My answer to that is that we have stipulated with the creditor that payment of duties shall be made in coin, and as long as the creditors shall have any possible interest in that, we have no right to change it. Now, as long as we redeem the notes in coin at New York he is not interested in demanding a strict fulfillment of that pledge, that we should collect our customs dues in coin, because he voluntarily waives it by receiving himself United States notes in lieu of that coin. I think, however, the stipulation in his favor ought to be left to protect him, and provide for any possible contingency of a change of circumstances.

Mr. FERRY. Is it your judgment that we should have this law continue on the statute books as long as there is a creditor of the government?

Secretary SHERMAN. If I had the power and were in the Senate with you gentlemen, making the laws, I should have no objection to the passage of this bill of Mr. Beck's, provided the simple amendment be added that while notes of the United States are redeemed according to law, they shall be receivable for all customs dues. With that qualification, I should vote for the bill with great pleasure. But I do not think it wise to surrender, by a repeal of that act, the stipulation in favor of the creditor.

Mr. FERRY. Then you desire to hold the power to deny the creditor the right to obtain gold for his greenback?

Secretary SHERMAN. No.

Mr. FERRY. But by including the words "while they are redeemed," you would continue to hold the power to deny the creditor, should he present his greenback for gold.

Secretary SHERMAN. This is a stipulation in favor of the bondholder that his interest shall be provided for out of a special fund. Now we simply say that as long as these United States notes are paid promptly in New York in coin, we should not be forced or asked to keep up this stipulation, and that is all we say; but that whenever it is for his interest, whenever we fail to redeem the notes according to the resumption act, we will then collect those duties in coin.

Mr. Ferry. That is, hold the power to deny the gold to the creditor upon his demand.

Secretary Sherman. That applies to both parties.

Mr. Ferry. For instance, he presents the greenback and demands payment in coin; if you see that your condition is such that in your judgment it ought not to be paid, you want the power to deny payment to him.

Secretary Sherman. You are thinking about the resumption act, and I am talking about the payment of customs dues in United States notes.

Mr. Ferry. But in case we are not meeting resumption—in case we cannot pay specie—you want to reserve the right to still receive coin for customs dues?

Secretary Sherman. Yes, because we have agreed to do that.

Mr. Ferry. Should we now, in a condition of prosperity, shield ourselves under a law passed in 1862, in our extremity? Should we not, when we are abundantly able, and ought to make good our promise to pay, make our paper equivalent to gold and receive it for customs dues and all other indebtedness? Ought we now, in a season of prosperity, to anticipate a time when we may be unable to pay gold for our greenbacks?

Secretary Sherman. I do not know but I have answered that by saying that I would do nothing about it. I would just let it stand as it is.

Mr. Ferry. That is the point?

Secretary Sherman. Yes, sir.

Mr. Allison. I want to ask you one further question. Would you regard it as a perfect compliance with the provisions of the law of 1862 to pass now a law whereby it should be provided that as long as these notes are actually redeemed in coin they shall be received for public dues? That would be no violation in your judgment of our contract with the creditor?

Secretary Sherman. No; I do not think it would.

Mr. Allison. I agree with you.

Secretary Sherman. I think that would be a substantial compliance with the contract. I do not think, however, it is very material any way, except that it is just as well for Congress to legislate upon this subject and tell me what shall be done. I would rather they would. I would rather some bill should be passed upon this subject, and I be given the direction of Congress, than to let this payment of customs dues in United States notes stand upon my order, which, as I told you before, I adopted only after full consideration and as a means of avoiding much inconvenience to the people.

Mr. Ferry. What injury would be done to the public creditors now to repeal the law of 1862?

Secretary Sherman. You cannot do that unless the creditors would consent; then we could repeal it.

Mr. Ferry. Our bonds are above par; all our obligations are above par, and what violation of an obligation would there be to a creditor under those circumstances?

Secretary Sherman. Senator Bayard answered that point in his speech the other day. That stipulation in the contract with the creditor continues until the last debt matures and is paid.

The Chairman. The note has been printed with that express exemption.

Mr. Ferry. And that act should continue in force until the last debt matures?

Secretary Sherman. Unless both parties, by mutual assent, or acquiescence, agree to a different course. No bondholder has ever complained of my course in reference to this matter of payment of customs dues with legal-tenders.

Mr. FERRY. At the same time you recognize the fact that the original takers of the bonds do not now hold them, but that they have passed into other hands?

Secretary SHERMAN. Yes, sir; and they are passing from hand to hand every day.

Mr. FERRY. And being above par, would naturally go into other hands?

Secretary SHERMAN. They are continually being transferred from hand to hand.

Mr. BECK. Section 3694 of the Revised Statutes reads thus:

SEC. 3694. The coin paid for duties on imported goods shall be set apart as a special fund, and shall be applied as follows:

First. To the payment in coin of the interest on the bonds and notes of the United States.

Second. To the purchase or payment of one per centum of the entire debt of the United States, to be made within each fiscal year, which is to be set apart as a sinking fund, and the interest of which shall in like manner be applied to the purchase or payment of the public debt, as the Secretary of the Treasury shall from time to time direct.

Third. The residue to be paid into the Treasury.

Has there been any change in that law of which you are aware?

Secretary SHERMAN. No, I think not; except so far as the resumption act may be held to modify it. I do not know of any other change.

Mr. BECK. That does not change anything as regards the receipts for customs.

Secretary SHERMAN. No, sir.

Mr. BECK. Then on what authority are you now receiving the legal-tender notes for customs dues?

Secretary SHERMAN. We receive the legal-tender notes in the nature of a coin-certificate—as a certificate of the United States of coin in the Treasury held for the payment of that note, thus treating legal-tender notes precisely as the law treats the coin-certificate. I ought to say the law you refer to was modified subsequently by providing for coin-certificates, which certificates are the representatives of coin in the Treasury, and are receivable by the express terms of the law for customs dues, and we consequently treat them in that way.

I will state that this point is more clearly set forth and more carefully expressed in the report I made in December, 1878, where I quoted this law and gave my reasons for believing that under the existing laws I could treat them as coin-certificates; and I was supported in that view by the Attorney-General, who thought the law fairly sustained me in so doing.

Mr. BECK. It is your opinion now that under the existing law, as sustained by the opinion of the Attorney-General, you have a right to receive legal-tender notes for customs?

Secretary SHERMAN. I think I have.

Mr. BECK. Then you regard the passage of a law authorizing them to be received for customs dues as unnecessary to give you any additional power?

Secretary SHERMAN. No; I think I have a right to receive them by the consent, express or implied, of both parties to the contract. While the United States notes are thus treated in the nature of a coin-certificate, it is a practical compliance with the law as long as the present state of affairs exists, but if the notes should for a moment fall below par I should deem it to be the duty of the Treasury at once to insist on the

payment of customs dues in coin, unless Congress in the mean time provided otherwise.

Mr. BECK. You propose, therefore, under the present condition of
things, to regard this law as now authorizing you to receive them, but
you are unwilling that there should be a law to require you to do so.
Is that the way I understand you?

Secretary SHERMAN. Yes; requiring me to do it under a different
state of facts than now exists.

Mr. BECK. What contract is there between any creditor of the government and any branch of the executive department of the government
relative to the receipt of legal-tender notes for customs dues? I am
not speaking now of the right of the creditor to demand payment in
coin, for he has a right to demand it.

Secretary SHERMAN. There is no other law except the law you have
read, taken in connection with the resumption act and the law providing for coin-certificates.

Mr. BECK. Have you copies of the orders that you issued to the custom-house officers directing them to receive legal-tender notes for customs dues?

Secretary SHERMAN. There were two orders issued; one concerning
the payment of interest in notes, the other the receipt of notes for customs dues. I hand you both.

Circular instructions concerning the resumption of specie payments.

1878.
Department No. 135.
Secretary's Office.

TREASURY DEPARTMENT,
Washington, D. C., December 14, 1878.

The following provision of law, and instructions thereunder, are published for the
information and guidance of all concerned:

"An act to provide for the resumption of specie payments.

* * * * * * *

"SECTION 3. * * * And on and after the first day of January, anno Domini eighteen hundred and seventy-nine, the Secretary of the Treasury shall redeem, in coin, the
United States legal-tender notes then outstanding, on their presentation for redemption at the office of the assistant treasurer of the United States in the city of New
York, in sums of not less than fifty dollars. * * *

"Approved January 14, 1875."

As the effect of the above section will be to remove any practical difference in the value
of coin and notes as a circulating medium after the first of January next, no distinction between them will be made in keeping, rendering, or settling the accounts of public officers, involving transactions which occur subsequently to that date.

Matured coupons of the United States, and checks issued by the Treasurer of the
United States for interest or principal of the public debt, by law payable in coin, will
be paid by the assistant treasurer of the United States at New York, upon presentation, in coin, or, if the claimant prefers, such coupons and checks will be paid by the
the said assistant treasurer, or by any other independent Treasury officer, in United
States notes.

Such registered interest, payable by law in coin, as is paid on schedules at any other
cities than New York will also be paid the claimant in coin, by check on the assistant
treasurer of the United States at New York, which check may be cashed in United
States notes if the holder prefer, or, if the claimant prefers, such interest may be paid
to him direct in United States notes by the officer charged with the payment of the
schedule.

Any check or draft hereafter drawn in payment of a public obligation, by law payable in coin, will have that fact plainly noted thereon.

JOHN SHERMAN,
Secretary.

10

Circular letter to officers of customs.

1878.
Department No. 141.
Secretary's Office.

TREASURY DEPARTMENT,
Washington, D. C., December 21, 1878.

Your attention is called to the provisions of the third section of the act of Congress approved January 14, 1875, providing that, on and after the first day of January, anno Domini eighteen hundred and seventy-nine, the Secretary of the Treasury shall redeem, in coin, the United States legal-tender notes then outstanding, on their presentation for redemption at the office of the assistant treasurer of the United States in the city of New York, in sums of not less than fifty dollars.

By reason of this act, you are authorized to receive United States notes, as well as gold coin and standard silver dollars, in payment of duties on imports on and after the first day of January, 1879.

Notes thus received will in every instance be deposited with the Treasurer, or some assistant treasurer of the United States, as are other collections of such duties, to be redeemed, from time to time, in coin, on government account, as the convenience of the service may demand.

JOHN SHERMAN,
Secretary.

———

Mr. BECK. The latter is the order concerning the receipt of notes for customs dues?

Secretary SHERMAN. Yes, sir.

Mr. BECK. I desire to know, Mr. Secretary, whether it is not better, in your opinion, that the Congress of the United States should prescribe the duties of executive officers, so that they can act in pursuance of ance of law rather than the executive officer should be acting on his own notions of what is best?

Secretary SHERMAN. I say yes, decidedly.

Mr. BECK. Is not that what we are proposing to do now by the passage of this law which I seek to have enacted, and are you not opposing that condition of things?

Secretary SHERMAN. An executive officer, when there is a doubt about the law, must give his own construction of it, but should of course readily conform to the action of Congress as soon as it is declared. The objection I make is not to the passage of a law, but that the bill as proposed applies it to a possible future state of affairs such as did not exist when this order was made and does not now.

Mr. BECK. Is it not to be presumed that the law-making power will be in session at least sufficiently often to make its laws conform to any existing exigency, and is it not fair to assume that Congress would do nearer what is right on its judgment than some Secretary would do on his judgment?

Secretary SHERMAN. My answer to that is this: I called the attention of Congress in December, 1878, to this condition of affairs, and receiving no dissent from the proposition that I made in the report at that time, in which I stated distinctly that in case Congress did not instruct me otherwise I would do so and so; and subsequently not receiving any objection, I issued this executive order. Now, if the Finance Committee or any portion of the Congress of the United States had expressed a doubt or taken any position upon the subject before the 1st of January, 1879, I would have withheld this order. But you did not, although I waited until you had adjourned for the holidays before issuing the order. That is all I can say. I had no doubt myself, and have not now, after the full examination which I made, that I might consider these United States notes as in the nature of coin-certificates and receive them for customs dues, but I do not object nor have I any feeling but that all laws must emanate from Congress, and that the executive officer has not the right to disregard the law.

Mr. BECK. I desire you to understand, Mr. Secretary, that I remember very well the very full statement made in your report of what you then said you were going to do, and I endeavored at that time to have a law passed to conform to what you desired. The bill which I have now pending is to enable you, and every other Secretary, to do exactly what you are doing and be protected by the law.

Secretary SHERMAN. I should rather you would do that by prescribing the exact terms under which these notes can be received for customs dues.

The CHAIRMAN. Have you considered that if a law were now passed making United States notes unconditionally receivable for duties on imports, it would be an infraction of the law of February 25, 1862, and the contract with the public creditors contained in it?

Secretary SHERMAN. I think it would; because it would not provide for a contingency that may happen. I repeat, however, that I would rather Congress, if it agrees with me that I did right in receiving these notes, should say so, and say how long it shall be continued. I think Congress owes it to the executive department. I think that Congress ought on this very delicate and important point to instruct the executive officer what to do, and if I were here I would feel it my duty to respond.

Mr. BECK. That was the sole object I had in trying to pass this bill, agreeing with the Secretary in the fact that it ought to be done. I desire to know whether or not in the present existing condition of things, with the large reduction in the public debt, the lowering of the interest, the accumulation of gold on hand, and the power the Secretary has to sell bonds *ad libitum*—for I believe that is the claim——

Secretary SHERMAN. Yes, sir.

The CHAIRMAN. Not quite *ad libitum*. He must sell them at par in gold, and he can only sell the bonds authorized under the act of 1870.

Mr. BECK. He can sell five per cent. bonds.

The CHAIRMAN. Of course, but only at par.

Mr. BECK. You can sell five per cent. bonds at par, *ad libitum*. Now, with all these favorable conditions, I ask you if there is any reasonable apprehension in your mind that any public creditor will be embarrassed in the collection of his interest by passing an act authorizing the legal-tender notes to be receivable for customs dues?

Secretary SHERMAN. I do not think so. I do not think there is any danger at present of that; but at the same time it is the public creditor, and not myself, who must decide that.

Mr. BECK. Has any public creditor complained at all of your action under the law since you have received legal-tender notes for customs dues?

Secretary SHERMAN. Not so far as I know, but some of the newspapers have complained of it as a stretch of executive authority.

Mr. BECK. But no public creditor has complained to you as the chief officer of the Treasury Department?

Secretary SHERMAN. O, no; none that I have ever heard of; indeed they are very glad to get the United States notes instead of gold.

Mr. BECK. Up to this time, is not the security of the national debt to the public creditor being increased: first, by reduction of the national debt; second, by at least a temporarily prosperous condition of things; and, third, by the increase of the property of the country?

Secretary SHERMAN. O, yes.

Mr. BECK. Is not the security increasing every day?

Secretary SHERMAN. Yes, sir; the security of the creditor is as absolutely sure as anything can be. Indeed I do not see how it can be any stronger.

Mr. BECK. I wish to say that I do not wish to violate any contract made with the public creditor; but I was in hopes we could pass a law making these notes receivable for customs dues without incurring any suspicion of bad faith, for I would not incur anything of that kind if I knew it. I remember in your last message, on page xii, you say, in speaking of the repeal of the legal-tender clause:

The Secretary, therefore, respectfully submits to Congress whether the legal-tender clause should not now be repealed as to all future contracts, and parties be left to stipulate the mode of payment. United States notes should still be receivable for all dues to the government, they should be promptly redeemed on demand, and ample provision made to secure such redemption.

I regarded that language as a recommendation under the existing condition of things—customs dues being a part of the dues to the government, and the language used being " should still be receivable for all dues to the Government"—that you would acquiesce in the passage of the bill I have offered.

Secretary SHERMAN. The language of the report was *eo presenti*, that they are now receivable.

Mr. BECK. You see the language would create the inference that I have given.

Secretary SHERMAN. That was extended to all future dues and justified that inference. I have no trouble or fear about those words being in your bill, but I do not want to give a shadow of a doubt to any public creditor of our purpose to violate the contract.

Mr. BECK. I understand you to say, then, that while you do not, as Secretary of the Treasury, desire to say anything from which any public creditor could for a moment suspect that you were diminishing, or endangering in any way, the security which he holds; that, judging from the past experience, the want of protest against it, the large security now held, and in your own opinion that there is no public debt better secured, you see no imminent danger in the passage of the law.

Secretary SHERMAN. O, no.

Mr. BECK. And a change of circumstances would have to occur before danger could arise ?

Secretary SHERMAN. Yes, sir. The passage of such a law might excite comment among public creditors abroad who are anxious to seize upon anything through which to cast reproach upon our people and government.

Mr. BECK. Still the fact remains that they have not done so since you have been acting upon this order ?

Secretary SHERMAN. Yes.

Mr. BECK. And our present condition is certainly better than when you began to receive notes for customs dues ?

Secretary SHERMAN. That is so.

Mr. FERRY. You replied to the chairman that the passage of a law authorizing the receivability of greenbacks for duties would be a violation of our obligation to the public creditor made in the act of 1862, requiring duties to be paid in coin.

Secretary SHERMAN. Yes, sir.

Mr. FERRY. If that be so, how do you reconcile your practice, under your order, of receiving greenbacks for duties, and consider it not to be a violation of our obligation under the law of 1862 ?

Secretary SHERMAN. That is expressly based upon the fact that we are now redeeming those notes in coin. As long as that condition of facts continues to exist we would maintain the order; but the very moment a different state of facts occurs we would change the order.

Mr. FERRY. If the practice under your order of receiving duties in these notes is not a breach of the obligation with the public creditor under the law of 1862, then, I ask, under present conditions, whether the enactment of a law authorizing you to receive them would be a violation of it. In other words, would a law directing you to receive them for dues be any more a violation of our obligations than your *order* directing your officers to receive them for dues ?

Secretary SHERMAN. Yes, sir; I think it would.

Mr. FERRY. To-day, under the present circumstances ?

Secretary SHERMAN. You must bear in mind that a law is a more permanent rule of action.

Mr. FERRY. It is repealable under different circumstances.

Secretary SHERMAN. It has a much more valid and authoritative sanction than an executive order.

Mr. FERRY. Any more than the fact that the receivability exists when you receive those notes for duties in the face of the law that requires them to be received in coin ? You say you construe them into coin-certificates; then, if to-day you construe them as coin-certificates, ought not a law to be passed declaring them coin-certificates ?

Secretary SHERMAN. I think I have answered that. That is a question which is rather within your province to decide than mine.

Mr. FERRY. I ask you, as an executive officer, whether you think the passage of a law such as is pending would be a violation of the obligations of the government; and if that be the case, tell me the difference, as I cannot perceive it, why is your order, or the practice under your order, any less a violation than a law authorizing you to do the very thing which is now being done?

Secretary SHERMAN. I think if you pass a law similar to my executive order there will be no objection; but that recites the fact that the notes are redeemable in coin, and are redeemed in coin. If you put it on that ground you might enact the law as you propose.

Mr. FERRY. That fact exists, and it is an acknowledged one throughout the country and the world, that not only are our greenbacks redeemable in coin but they are redeemed in coin. You remarked that the creditor preferred to take the greenback to coin when they are equivalent. Upon that state of facts to-day—and of course we cannot suppose that it would change in the course of a week, the time necessary to pass a law—why would it be any more a violation of our obligations to pass a law authorizing you to do the very thing you are doing under an order ? That is the point which I cannot reconcile my mind to.

Secretary SHERMAN. If you pass a law in the language of this order, it would remove all my objections :

Notes thus received will in every instance be deposited with the Treasurer or some assistant treasurer of the United States, as are other collections of such duties, to be redeemed from time to time in coin on government account, as the convenience of the service may demand.

When we receive these notes they are practically redeemed in one sense, and we so keep the accounts and treat them as notes redeemed in coin. If they are not at the time redeemable or redeemed in coin, the whole basis upon which this order is founded will fall.

Mr. FERRY. Suppose I were a bondholder (which I am not) and you authorize your officers to receive the greenbacks for customs dues ; now,

I have not given my consent to that; the fact that you say afterwards in your order that this is to be a matter of regulation and that they are finally to be redeemed in coin, does not relieve you of my claim upon the government that the duty shall be received in coin, in order that the interest on my bonds should be paid? If that is the requirement of the law, why should any practice violate it—that is, by a non compliance? I do not speak of violation in any offensive sense at all. If under an order you do a thing under the present state of facts, why is it objectionable that a law should be passed authorizing you to do the very same thing? That other matter—the last paragraph—is a regulation to the Treasurer; it goes into your treasury vault, and is simply a transfer from one account to another.

Secretary SHERMAN. Here is the actual fact: These notes may have been presented to the Assistant Treasurer at the sub-treasury, situated on one side of Wall street, for payment in coin, the coin paid and carried over across the street to the collector at the custom-house to liquidate the duties, and from there carried back to the sub-treasury, and deposited to the credit of the custom-house officer, and all that must be done on the same day. We simply say that we will receive these notes from these people who are paying customs dues, and present them at the sub-treasury for redemption—that is, we will carry over the notes instead of the coin, and the sub-treasury will give us credit as coin.

Mr. FERRY. Is there any law to do that?

Secretary SHERMAN. No express law.

Mr. FERRY. You assume to do that transaction for their convenience, which the law does not authorize you to do in my judgment.

Secretary SHERMAN. There was the fact.

Mr. FERRY. Your order is universal, and you may apply it to San Francisco in the same way.

Secretary SHERMAN. Yes, sir. The order extends throughout the United States.

Mr. ALLISON. If I understand you, it is your judgment that where any promise has been made to any public creditor, that promise should be kept in its full spirit and intent.

Secretary SHERMAN. Yes, sir.

Mr. ALLISON. Although its violation might not involve any real loss; and it is for that reason that you object to an absolute abrogation of this act of 1862.

The CHAIRMAN. Unconditional?

Mr. ALLISON. Unconditional. But I understand you not to object to a provision which would authorize you to receive these notes for customs dues as long as they are actually redeemed as now provided in the resumption act.

Secretary SHERMAN. No; I should be very glad if that were done.

Mr. ALLISON. You think that would be in no sense a violation of our contract with the public creditor under the act of 1862?

Secretary SHERMAN. I do not see how it could be. It might be the most technical and barren change in the contract, but it would not be a substantial one.

Mr. ALLISON. Though it was no more than that you think it ought not to be done.

Secretary SHERMAN. Yes.

Senator ALLISON. Now suppose, as between Chicago and New York, for example, the exchange should be adverse to Chicago—that is, suppose a Treasury note in Chicago should be at one-half per cent. discount as compared with gold, that it cost one-half per cent. to convert the paper into coin in New York, and because of that difference in the exchange between those two cities the United States notes or Treasury note, or whatever it may be, should fall one-half per cent. below par—would you then feel that you could receive it in payment for customs dues?

Secretary SHERMAN. Certainly. Such a case as that you suppose is not probable; but still I would receive it as long as the goverment continued to redeem it at New York in coin. Because hogs are very abundant and money in very urgent demand at Cincinnati or Chicago, thus causing a variation in exchange, we cannot change our rules.

Mr. ALLISON. But you would still receive for customs dues an obligation of the Government which was at the point of receipt a half per cent. below the coin.

Secretary SHERMAN Undoubtedly I would; for the resumption act treats resumption in New York as resumption everywhere in the country, and I would consequently do the same. In fact, it is always so.

Mr. ALLISON. Would you make any difference.

Secretary SHERMAN. I would make no difference. We do not now. United States notes are at a premium over gold everywhere, except in New York.

Mr ALLISON. You say they are at a premium?

Secretary SHERMAN. There is a shade of difference. That is, the notes are preferred; and they are preferred in New York even.

Senator FERRY. The cost of transportation creates that difference in their favor?

Secretary SHERMAN. Yes; we issued an order some time since, in which we required the party ordering specie to pay transportation charges, and it created a great deal of complaint.

Senator FERRY. Your difficulty now, in New York even, is in supplying United States notes, not in supplying coin?

Secretary SHERMAN. That is so. But the surplus of coin put us in that condition. We had to pay out coin (and I was compelled to issue a peremptory order to that effect) in very large amounts, because we had not United States notes enough to meet the demand.

Mr. FERRY. Then the tendency now, as I understand it, is for coin to flow into the Treasury and not out of it?

Secretary SHERMAN. Yes, sir.

Mr. FERRY. How long has that continued?

Secretary SHERMAN. Since the 1st of July; and I think to a very slight extent since the 1st of January, 1879.

The CHAIRMAN. You have not sold any bonds since resumption, except for refunding?

Secretary SHERMAN. We have not sold any bonds for resumption since resumption commenced.

Mr. ALLISON. Is it not a fact that the tendency of coin has been into the Treasury, and not out of it?

Secretary SHERMAN. Yes, sir; since resumption we could, if we had kept all the gold coin and bullion that came into the Treasury in the ordinary course of business, have had now over $200,000,000.

Mr. ALLISON. You stated in the beginning of your remarks that you had $148,000,000 of coin reserve over and above all liabilities. Do you mean by that, that you have $148,000,000 of coin now applicable to the redemption of United States notes?

Secretary SHERMAN. Yes, sir; over and above all other liabilities. That reserve is a little larger now, however, than it will be, because there is some interest accruing not yet due, and some surplus revenue which in due course will be paid for bonds for the sinking fund, leaving, however, a net resumption fund of about $135,000,000.

Mr. ALLISON. Do you now issue coin certificates?

Secretary SHERMAN. Yes; we issue silver certificates, but no gold certificates.

Mr. ALLISON. You do not issue any coin certificates under the provisions which you alluded to a while ago?

Secretary SHERMAN. No.

Mr. ALLISON. Your mode of accumulating coin is to exchange greenbacks for coin instead of for coin certificates?

Secretary SHERMAN. The coin comes into the Treasury most of it through the mints, where bullion goes for coinage. A large acquisition of coin has come from foreign lands, and has been taken to the assay office to be melted, and then finally paid for by the Treasurer in United States notes.

Mr. ALLISON. You remarked also that, in addition to this coin reserve which you have of $148,000,000, you regarded your power as ample and complete to sell 5 per cent. bonds at not less than par in coin for the purpose of maintaining these notes at par.

Secretary SHERMAN. Yes; 4 per cents, 4½ per cents, or 5 per cents.

Mr. ALLISON. Just whichever one of these three classes of bonds you please; and the only restriction upon you is that you are not to sell them at less than par in coin?

Secretary SHERMAN. That is the law.

Mr. ALLISON. So that your means after all are ample and complete for maintaining these notes at par in coin?

Secretary SHERMAN. Yes, sir; and I think it is better to have them ample, because the fact that this power does exist is a great protection to resumption, and it is a kind of power that no public officer would dare to abuse; for he would be at once assailed by everybody.

Mr. ALLISON. I have no doubt about that. It is just as complete as though you had $500,000,000 of 5 per cent. bonds set apart as a particular fund in the Treasury to redeem those notes.

Secretary SHERMAN. Certainly.

Senator BECK. Desiring of course, as I do, to see legal-tender notes received for all customs dues, I wish to ask you if the present action of the Treasury Department in receiving them in that way, as it now does, is not liable to be reversed by any Secretary who may succeed you and take a more limited view of his powers under the law?

Secretary SHERMAN. Certainly

Mr. BECK. And is not that in itself an uncertainty?

Secretary SHERMAN. Any order made by a department could be reversed, except in certain cases of tariff dues.

Mr. BECK. And therefore that uncertainty hangs now over the continuance of the receipt of these notes for customs dues.

Secretary SHERMAN. Any Secretary may reverse that order. I could do it myself, and any other succeeding Secretary might do it.

Mr. BECK. Yes; but I am not apprehensive that you are about to do it.

Secretary SHERMAN. Certainly not.

Mr. BECK. I am speaking of the uncertainty of the existing condition of things under that order—its being subject to reversal by you or by any successor you might have. Is not the tendency, through the receipt of legal-tenders for customs dues, to appreciate their value, first, by reason of the convenience; second, because a merchant of San Francisco, or Saint Paul, or any remote point, being able to procure gold in New York only, finds it much more convenient to use legal-tender notes?

Secretary SHERMAN. Undoubtedly that gives them more circulation.

Mr. BECK. And, with one point to redeem at, is not the convenience a great deal to the merchant to pay in notes?

Secretary SHERMAN. Certainly. We do not redeem United States notes except in New York, because we have to obey the law; but we pay out gold and silver everywhere on current obligations.

Mr. BECK. You say that the receipt of these notes for customs dues gives them a shade of additional value because it gives them additional use.

Secretary SHERMAN. They are more convenient to use.

Mr. BECK. Any additional use, of course, has a tendency to enhance the value of those notes.

Secretary SHERMAN. That is true.

Mr. FERRY. There is just one question that came up to my mind by the reply of the Secretary that he could change his own order; it brought to my mind this question: If you should, as you have the right to, reverse your order permitting the greenbacks to be received for duties, then the bondholder holds his rights against the Government of the United States—payment to him of interest and the payment of principal of his bonds—subject to executive order. If you can reverse this order which permits greenbacks to be received for duties at any time, are his rights protected?

Secretary SHERMAN. The creditor could not be possibly injured by the receipt of United States notes for customs dues as long as they are redeemed in coin. It is not presumed that the creditor any more than anybody else would be a fool and would object to that which was so greatly to the public benefit and not to his injury.

Senator FERRY. Let me cite a case that might occur: Having the secrets of the administration, you might apprehend war; there might be reasons that would appear to you which would not appear to any other person, and having that in charge, you might reverse this order. Would not that be a violation of the rights of the creditor of the government before the justification was apparently public; and would it not be more liable under an executive order changeable at pleasure than under a law which would require an act of Congress to reverse it?

Secretary SHERMAN. Well, I do not know that I see the point.

Mr. ALLISON. The order is reversed for the protection of the creditor.

Mr. FERRY. It changes the relations, whether it is to be done by executive order or by law. It is simply that point. I cannot possibly see the difference as to the violation of the obligation with the creditor between the passage of a law that authorizes the same fact and an executive order which reaches the same end. In other words, you order that greenbacks be received for dues, and yet you are opposed to the passage of a law to do the same thing.

Secretary SHERMAN. Unless the law provides, as I have provided in this order, that it shall only be done while the redemption of the United States notes continues; with that modification I have no objection to the bill at all.

Mr. BECK. Have you made any orders for the payment of gold and silver and for their issue in disbursements?

Secretary SHERMAN. Yes, sir, I have; here is my order of October 8, 1879.

The CHAIRMAN. Is that in the printed book?

2 SH

Secretary SHERMAN. No, it is the Treasurer's order; but the order directing it and the reasons given are in the printed book; here it is.

TREASURY OF THE UNITED STATES,
Washington, October 8, 1879.

SIR: It is the practice in this office to pay in coin twenty per cent. the amount of current obligations of the government presented—ten per cent. in standard silver dollars and ten per cent. in gold coin.

At the suggestion of the Secretary you are hereby instructed to make, in like proportion, payment of current obligations of the government in silver and gold, giving to the payee in payment of the balance gold or silver coin, if desired by him. The ten per cent. in standard silver dollars should be furnished to United States disbursing officers in actual coin; to private parties, banks, &c., payment may be made either in silver dollars or silver certificates. Silver certificates will be sent you upon application to the Treasurer. This letter is not intended to affect any existing arrangement with the clearing-house.

Very respectfully,

JAS. GILFILLAN,
Treasurer United States.

Hon. THOMAS HILLHOUSE,
Assistant Treasurer United States, New York.

[NOTE.—" Similar instructions, excepting the clause relating to the clearing-house, sent to all other sub-treasury offices."]

The CHAIRMAN. Then it amounted to the resumption of the payment of gold and silver in full, if any one desired it; or whether they desired it or not, it was a compulsory payment, excepting at the clearing-house, of twenty per cent. in gold and silver, and that was an equal payment of each, all over the country?

Secretary SHERMAN. Yes, sir.

The CHAIRMAN. Does that apply to every disbursing agent of the government?

Secretary SHERMAN. Every assistant treasurer, and, consequently, every disbursing officer, because the sub-treasurers pay out the money to the disbursing officers and pay them according to the directions in this order.

The CHAIRMAN. The object of that order was very obvious; it was to diffuse and put in circulation the gold and silver coin.

Secretary SHERMAN. It was because we were comparatively short of United States notes and had plenty of gold and silver.

The CHAIRMAN. The notes were not in the Treasury and this coin was there, and you paid it out in this way and gave this order so that you should not be short of United States notes?

Secretary SHERMAN. Yes, sir.

Mr. BECK. Do I understand you to say that in these orders you required persons to whom interest on the public debt was due to take 20 per cent. in coin.

Secretary SHERMAN. There was no distinction in that matter.

Mr. BECK. And did you do that?

Secretary SHERMAN. We did.

Mr. BECK. And required them to take it?

Secretary SHERMAN. Except this: the great body of our interest is paid by checks on New York, and as a matter of convenience they are usually collected through the clearing-house. We do that for our own convenience, because it would be a very expensive operation for the government to transport the coin necessary to pay the interest on the debt to the different places; therefore, as a rule, we pay in drafts on New York.

Mr. ALLISON. That is, on registered bonds?

Secretary SHERMAN. Yes, sir. The Treasurer also issues checks on New York for coupons presented for payment.

Mr. ALLISON. Before passing from that order I wish to ask you a question : I understand you that your order was made because of the great accumulation of coin in the Treasury ?

Secretary SHERMAN. Yes, sir.

Mr. ALLISON. And because you did not have enough United States notes to meet the demand ?

Secretary SHERMAN. The table which I have here will show that fact.

Mr. ALLISON. I want it to show on the record so that it is perfectly clear.

Secretary SHERMAN. O, yes, of course, that is perfectly clear. If anybody wanted the whole paid in coin he could obtain it.

Mr. ALLISON. But it was a compulsory payment of twenty per cent. in coin ?

The CHAIRMAN. Compulsory reception.

Mr. ALLISON. As I understand, it was a compulsory payment; he compelled everybody to take coin in lieu of paper as a payment on the part of the Treasurer ?

The CHAIRMAN. Yes, sir.

Secretary SHERMAN. The monthly statement will come out to-morrow, and I will take the liberty of embodying it in the report of these proceedings.

Statement of liabilities and assets of the Treasury of the United States from latest returns received.

Liabilities.

Fund for redemption of certificates of deposit, June 6, 1872		$12,900,000 00
Post-Office Department account		2,773,144 41
Disbursing officers' balances		19,634,898 33
Fund for redemption of notes of national banks "failed," "in liquidation," and "reducing circulation"		16,339,015 25
Undistributed assets of failed national banks		635,307 17
Five per cent. fund for redemption of national-bank notes		15,611,620 51
Fund for redemption of national-bank gold notes		234,220 00
Currency and minor-coin redemption account		3,940 02
Fractional silver-coin redemption account		85,364 25
Interest account		196,505 36
Interest account, Pacific Railroads and Louisville and Portland Canal Company		22,960 00
Treasurer United States, agent for paying interest on District of Columbia bonds		491,150 97
Treasurer's transfer checks outstanding		3,279,726 31
Treasurer's general account, interest due and unpaid	$9,654,223 49	
Treasurer's general account, called bonds and interest	12,104,943 69	
Treasurer's general account, old debt	831,585 07	
Treasurer's general account, gold certificates	10,411,100 00	
Treasurer's general account, silver certificates	9,052,910 00	
Treasurer's general account, refunding certificates	2,069,800 00	
Treasurer's general account, balance, including bullion fund		141,410,632 48
		193,535,304 73
		265,795,277 31

Assets.

Gold coin and bullion	$153,690,036 43
Standard silver dollars	34,961,611 00
Fractional silver coin	20,204,599 83
Silver bullion	4,888,035 97
Gold certificates	61,100 00
Silver certificates	5,063,456 00
United States notes	24,299,562 45
National-bank notes	6,671,216 48
National-bank gold notes	214,730 00
Fractional currency	85,358 75
Deposits held by national-bank depositories	10,830,840 42
Nickel and minor coin	1,341,708 10
New York and San Francisco exchange	2,131,000 00
One and two year notes, &c.	147 00
Redeemed certificates of deposits, June 8, 1872	215,000 00
Quarterly interest checks and coin coupons paid	401,999 12
Registered and unclaimed interest paid	25,061 75
United States bonds and interest	507 64
Interest on District of Columbia bonds	5,674 07
Deficits, unavailable funds	690,848 30
Speaker's certificates	12,510 00
Pacific Railroad interest paid	
	265,795,277 31

JAMES GILFILLAN,
Treasurer United States.

TREASURY OF THE UNITED STATES,
Washington, D. C., February 2, 1880.

Mr. BECK. What I desired in this whole matter was to obtain your views fully, and then let Congress, after an examination of your statements, decide whether it is better to have an executive order or a law on the subject. I believe in a law in preference to an order.

EXCHANGE OF TRADE-DOLLARS.

Mr. BECK. I have introduced several bills to facilitate the exchange of trade for standard dollars.

Secretary SHERMAN. The bill which I have here is a House bill. There is no objection in my mind to the object of this bill; that is, to provide for the exchange of the trade-dollar for the standard silver dollar; the only point is whether the trade-dollar shall be treated as bullion or as a coined dollar of the United States. Now, I am clearly of the opinion that it ought to be treated as so much bullion issued at the expense of merchants for their convenience and benefit, and without profit to the United States, and therefore not entitled to any preference over other bullion, and we might say not to so much, because it was issued to private parties for their benefit and at their cost, but stamped by us merely to enable the coins to be used to better advantage in a foreign market. I have not, therefore, any objection to the bill if you allow us to pay the same for these trade-dollars as for other bullion.

Mr. WALLACE. You have that authority now under the present law.

Mr. FERRY. Will you have the bill read as it was amended in the committee?

That the Secretary of the Treasury shall cause to be exchanged, at the Treasury and at all sub-treasuries of the United States, legal-tender silver dollars for trade-dollars at their market value, regarded as bullion; and shall recoin the said trade dollars into legal-tender dollars, as now provided by law; and shall stop the further coinage of trade-dollars: *Provided,* That trade-dollars that have been "chopped" or restamped for circulation in China or other foreign countries shall be excluded from the provisions of this act.

Mr. FERRY. That is providing for the purchase of trade dollars at their market rate as bullion.

Secretary SHERMAN. That is it.

Mr. BECK. Is there not a good deal of hardship that a dollar like that, with seven and a half more grains of silver in it than the standard dollar, in the hands of the people all over the country, taking it and believing it to be a dollar; and is it not a shame, for the little margin of profit to the government, to have complaints made that we are depreciating it and buying it cheaper? Had we not better take it in exchange for standard dollars?

Secretary SHERMAN. I would say that there are five or six millions of trade-dollars in the country at the present time, and by that method of redemption it would cost the government about a million dollars; that would be one objection; but the great bulk of these trade-dollars has gone abroad, and they amount in the aggregate to some thirty-four or thirty-five millions. We have official information that they are not chopped; that they are held by the Hong-Kong and China merchants, who keep them as bullion and count them as bullion; but the very moment you give them this factitious value they would be brought back again to this country, and speculated upon for the profit which would accrue from the difference between their real and factitious values. I really believe if you would attempt to do that you would stop the purchase of silver bullion and do much damage.

Mr. BECK. And you think that the inconvenience caused by the few that are here would be much less than the loss sustained through the return of those now held abroad ?

Secretary SHERMAN. They have a certain value for shipment abroad, and they are very often nearly at par in San Francisco. I think it is better for the people to lose this little percentage than to have the whole of this mass thrown upon us.

The CHAIRMAN. I have noticed the sales of a quantity in San Francisco at 99½ cents, for shipment to China.

Mr. ALLISON. They have been at that figure in New York.

Secretary SHERMAN. Then there is no harm done; but if you pass a law requiring us to pay 100 cents for silver bullion worth 89 cents, it is a loss of over 10 per cent. on the whole mass.

Mr. WALLACE. What would be the objection to allowing an exchange of them for subsidiary coin in limited amounts ?

Secretary SHERMAN. That would amount to the same thing. We have already over nineteen millions of the subsidiary coin loading us down, and we do not want any more. That will be absorbed after a while.

The CHAIRMAN. How much fractional coin have you on hand ?

Secretary SHERMAN. About twenty millions.

Mr. BECK. That is not all there is ?

Secretary SHERMAN. We have that amount in the Treasury. Fourteen millions of that came back through redemptions after the law of last session was passed, and of that fourteen millions redeemed over 20 per cent. was of coin dated before the war, which had been hoarded in stockings and scattered in foreign countries, and which had come back to be redeemed.

The CHAIRMAN. In multiples of twenty dollars.

Secretary SHERMAN. We have, I see by referring to the tables, $19,972,000 on hand now ; when your law passed authorizing the redemption with legal tenders we had about six millions.

Mr. WALLACE. There would be no objection to the taking it in amounts of twenty dollars in exchange for the trade dollars.

Secretary SHERMAN. That would give them ten per cent. profit, and it would result in bringing all the trade-dollars back into the country. That subsidiary coin would get into circulation and must be redeemed again. The only way we can keep this money—the silver dollar and the subsidiary coin—at par with the greenback and gold is by always freely receiving it; therefore, I approved of your order of last session. It is our policy not to force them out unwillingly, but to use every possible proper means to circulate them.

Mr. FERRY. As subsidiary to that object, and to keep the silver dollar at par, would it not be wise to retire all the small bills under five dollars and make room for more silver ?

Secretary SHERMAN. I am not ready to propose that. Perhaps some of the rest are.

Mr. BECK. Is that substantially what you desire to say about the exchange of the trade-dollar ?

Secretary SHERMAN. I desire to say that in an interview with a committee of the House, embodied in this document which I hold in my hand, the whole question about the subsidiary coin and the silver trade-dollar was gone over, and they published this, which is a very full statement.

(See appendix A.)

Mr. BECK. Have you any other special suggestions in addition to these ? We would be glad to have them.

The CHAIRMAN. This is a pretty full statement.

Secretary SHERMAN. This was made when it was fresh matter and it was fully discussed.

Mr. FERRY. In speaking in reply to a question of mine in reference to the retirement of small bills under five dollars, you said you were not a bold enough man to propose it. Will you give your opinion as to the propriety of it?

Secretary SHERMAN. Well, I do not see any object to attain. Such a retirement would put a certain class of people to great inconvenience. The small bills are so convenient to send by mail; especially would the publishers of newspapers be inconvenienced. I do not see any great object to be accomplished by forcing silver into circulation by such means.

Mr. FERRY. Would not the inconvenience be remedied by the use of the money-order system?

Secretary SHERMAN. The expense of that is an objection.

'Mr. FERRY. Would it not open channels for some twenty to twenty-five millions of silver to circulate in?'

Secretary SHERMAN. It might.

Mr. FERRY. To meet the retirement of these notes?

Secretary SHERMAN. What use would it be to us to force silver out, when we can just as well issue United States notes?

Mr. FERRY. The object is to make it equivalent; and if they are to run together, you have the fact right before the people in their daily practice that we are continuing to resume; one is the equivalent of the other. If by the regulations of the Treasury or by practice there is no silver in circulation, and you find difficulty in getting it out, by this method you would open a channel for $25,000,000 more. If it is not out, then the currency takes its place; if it is out, it makes that much more room for currency—that is, it gives a greater volume of currency, because you hold about so much reserve in the Treasury; if silver was not there, currency would be.

Secretary SHERMAN. It strikes me that the better way is to let everybody have just what kind of money he chooses. Make the different kinds of currency equal to each other, and give every man his choice. You may have greenbacks, gold and silver in various forms, and national-bank bills, but let the gold and silver coin be the standard of value to measure everything else, and maintain the others at par in that coin, letting every man choose what he shall be paid in. I do not believe it will do to attempt to draw in these small bills.

Mr. FERRY. I thought it would be a means of distributing the silver.

REPEAL OF LEGAL-TENDER CLAUSE.

The CHAIRMAN. The next proposition is

"The effect the abolition of the legal-tender quality of the greenbacks will have on our paper currency."

Mr. BECK. I said in my note that I would inquire into the effect the abolition of the legal-tender quality of the greenbacks will have on our paper currency. The question is a long one, but I desire to get the Secretary's views upon it. I will read section 3588 of the Revised Statutes, which is in these words:

United States notes shall be lawful money, and a legal tender in payment of all debts, public and private, within the United States, except for dues on imports and interest on the public debt.

Section 5182 provides, in regard to the national-bank notes, this:

After any association receiving circulating notes under this Title has caused its promise to pay such notes on demand to be signed by the president or vice-president and cashier thereof, in such manner as to make them obligatory promissory notes, payable on demand, at its place of business, such association may issue and circulate the same as money. And the same shall be received at par in all parts of the United States in payment of taxes, excises, public lands, and all other dues to the United States, except duties on imports; and also for all salaries and other debts and demands owing by the United States to individuals, corporations, and associations within the United States, except interest on the public debt, and in redemption of the national currency

Section 5196 is as follows:

Every national banking association formed or existing under this Title, shall take and receive at par, for any debt or liability to it, any and all notes or bills issued by any lawfully organized national banking association. But this provision shall not apply to any association organized for the purpose of issuing notes payable in gold.

Now, the resolution which the Senate is considering, which is substantially the recommendation of the Secretary, I believe, is that from and after the passage of this resolution all United States notes shall be receivable for all dues to the United States except duties on imports, and shall not be otherwise a legal tender. My object is to ask the Secretary whether, in case his recommendation and the present resolution become a law, the Treasury Department will have any power to require any person to receive legal-tender notes in liquidation of any obligations or liabilities of the United States, and whether or not national-bank notes will not, after its passage, by retaining the powers they now have, be the only paper money the government or individuals can require any person to accept.

The CHAIRMAN. Do you suppose that there is now any compulsory legal-tender power attached?

Mr. BECK. Yes, sir.

Mr. ALLISON. It is complete. You are bound to take them for your salary to-day.

Mr. BECK. Every national-bank note is a legal tender to you by the government and you cannot help it.

The CHAIRMAN. I very much doubt that.

Mr. BECK. My question is whether there will be any power to require any person to receive legal-tender notes in satisfaction of any obligations or liabilities of the United States, and whether or not national-bank notes will not, after the passage of this resolution, by retaining their powers, be the only paper money the government or individuals can require any person to accept.

Secretary SHERMAN. So far as the general theory of making a legal tender of the United States note, now that we have attained resumption, is concerned, I desire to say that in my annual report I have stated my views in reference thereto as carefully and fully as I possibly could. What I said in that report is as full and fair a statement of my views as I can possibly give now. I reproduce it:

The Secretary respectfully calls the attention of Congress to the question whether United States notes ought still to be a legal tender in the payment of debts. The power of Congress to make them such was asserted by Congress during the war, and was upheld by the Supreme Court. The power to reissue them in time of peace, after they are once redeemed, is still contested in that court. Prior to 1862 only gold and silver were a legal tender. Bullion was deposited by private individuals in the mints and coined in convenient forms and designs, indicating weight and fineness. Paper money is a promise to pay such coin. No constitutional objection is raised against the issue of notes not bearing interest to be used as a part of the circulating medium. The chief objection to the emission of paper-money by the government grows out of the legal-tender clause, for without this the United States note would be measured by its convenience in use, its safety, and its prompt redemption. In war, and during a grave public exigency, other considerations may properly prevail; but it would seem that during peace and especially during times of prosperity and surplus revenue, the promissory note of the United States ought to stand like any other promissory note. It should be current money only by being promptly redeemed in coin on demand. The note of the United States is now received for all public dues, it is carefully limited in amount, it is promptly redeemed on demand, and ample reserves in coin are provided to give confidence in and security for such redemption. With these conditions maintained, the United States note will be readily received and paid on all demands. While they are maintained, the legal-tender clause gives no additional credit or sanction to the notes, but tends to impair confidence and to create fears of overissue. It would seem, therefore, that now and during the maintenance of resumption it is a useless and objectionable assertion of power, which Congress might now repeal on the ground of expediency alone. When it is considered that its constitutionality is seriously contested, and that from its nature it is subject to grave abuse, it would now appear to be wise to withdraw the exercise of such a power, leaving it in reserve to be again resorted to in such a period of war or grave emergency as existed in 1862. The Government derives an advantage in circulating its notes without interest, and the people prefer such notes to coin, as money, for their convenience in use and their certain redemption in coin on demand. This mutual advantage may be secured without the exercise of questionable power; nor need any inconvenience arise from the repeal of the legal-tender clause as to future contracts. Contracting parties may stipulate for either gold or silver coin or current money. In the absence of an express stipulation for coin, the reasonable presumption would exist that the parties contemplated payment in current money, and such presumption might properly be declared by law and the contract enforced accordingly.

The Secretary, therefore, respectfully submits to Congress whether the legal-tender clause should not now be repealed as to all future contracts, and parties be left to stipulate the mode of payment. United States notes should still be receivable for all dues to the government, they should be promptly redeemed on demand, and ample provision made to secure such redemption.

Mr. BECK. I was not asking for that now, because you have already given it. I simply ask whether, if that resolution or your recommendation become a law, the United States will have power to require any person to take United States notes, or whether the government will have any power to issue them at all, and whether the national-bank notes, through the power given by the sections I have recited, will not remain the only paper money that any person can be required to pay or take.

Secretary SHERMAN. The question presented by you is one rather of construction of the bill of Mr. Bayard, upon which, as a matter of delicacy, it would not be exactly right for me to enter; but I certainly am not in favor of any bill that will give to the national-bank note any quality, use, or value that is not given to the United States note. Indeed, I would give to the United States note every quality, attribute, or use that can be given to it by Congress without trenching upon questionable and dangerous powers, such as that of making a promise to pay money—actual money—in contracts between private individuals.

Mr. BECK. My question was, What power the United States will have to *require* any person to take any of its notes?

Secretary SHERMAN. The United States as a creditor has the undoubted power to say what it will receive in payment of that which is due its own. It may take notes or bank notes, as it chooses. The repeal of the legal-tender clause, in my judgment, would not affect any provision of the bank law at all. Nor will it have any effect upon the use or convenience or negotiability of the United States notes, except it will take away from them that forced power by which a promise to pay money is made a substitute for actual money when the creditor is not willing to receive it. I do not think that after resumption it is a power necessary to the credit of United States notes, and I think it is a very questionable power on the part of Congress to make a promise to pay money an actual legal tender in payment of debts. If it was perfectly clear, and if I did not think it was a question that would constantly be contested before the courts, I should have no objection to the legal-tender quality of the notes continuing, at least as long as they are redeemed at sight in coin, for I favor the issue and circulation of United States notes as lawful money and would give them every attribute desirable and lawful for that purpose; but now, as they are subject to doubt, that question will be continually arising, and as the legal-tender attribute given to the notes is of no value and does not add to their circulation, I am in favor of taking it away.

Mr. BECK. You have said that in your report very well; but the question remains, which I put very distinctly: If your recommendations or this resolution should be adopted, what power, if any, will the United States have to issue any of these United States notes?

Secretary SHERMAN. O, well, there is no question as to the power of the United States to issue its notes, and, so far as they are willing to be taken as money, there can be no question of power raised. The only question of power that ever was raised about them was as to the legal-tender quality.

Mr. BECK. After the legal-tender quality is taken away, has the United States the power left to make any human being take one of them?

Mr. MORRILL. That is simply asking whether, after the legal-tender quality is repealed, it will exist.

Mr. BECK. I repeat my question: Under those circumstances would the United States have the power to make any human being take one of them?

Secretary SHERMAN. I say yes. It has the same power to make every person take United States notes that it has to make them take bank notes; but it has no power, as it is claimed, to make any one, as a compulsory matter, take United States notes or bank notes. It never has undertaken to make the bank note a legal tender in payment of debts. It has provided certain cases where they may be received or paid.

Mr. BECK. I repeat my question: What power has the United States, after the legal-tender quality is taken away from these notes, to require any person or corporation to take them, with that legal-tender quality destroyed?

Secretary SHERMAN. It has the power to prescribe what it will pay its officers. It has the power to prescribe what it will receive for dues of every character. It has the power to declare these notes lawful money, and that all contracts which do not prescribe on their face coin payments shall be held to be payable in such money. The only doubt about the power of Congress is whether it can say that a promise to pay a dollar is an actual dollar.

Mr. BECK. The question now before the Senate reads, "That they. shall be receivable for all dues to the United States, except duties on imports, and shall not otherwise be a legal tender." I ask you, provided that becomes a law, what power the United States has to require any person to take any of those notes for anything?

Mr. KERNAN. Your question is, I suppose, who could they make take them?

Mr. ALLISON. Assuming that resolution to pass.

Mr. BECK. Who could the United States make take them, assuming that to be the law? Is there any power remaining in the United States to make any person take them at all?

Secretary SHERMAN. Well, I cannot answer that more clearly than I have already.

The CHAIRMAN. It answers itself.

Secretary SHERMAN. Obligations incurred prior to the passage of the proposed law should be excepted.

Mr. BECK. I am assuming that those obligations have been paid. Can they then make any person take them?

Secretary SHERMAN. The law might provide that they shall be received in all payments to or from the government not otherwise provided for.

Mr. BECK. But I am not asking that, Mr. Secretary.

Mr. ALLISON. I have a curiosity to know your opinion about that myself, Mr. Secretary.

Secretary SHERMAN. This resolution has been introduced by Senator Bayard, and I would probably seek to amend it.

Mr. BECK. The resolution is up before us now for consideration, and I ask you, if that becomes a law just as it is proposed there, would there be any power left in the United States to require me, as a member of Congress, or any person to whom the United States owes money, to take United States notes?

The CHAIRMAN. I hope not.

Mr. BECK. I ask you that question on the supposition that this resolution becomes a law.

Secretary SHERMAN. If it becomes a law in its present form, it would repeal all these clauses which authorize the notes to be paid for any class of debts.

Mr. BECK. That is what I ask you.

Secretary SHERMAN. That is what the Senator intends, I have no doubt; but my impression is that a repeal of the legal-tender clause, as I understand it, would not have that effect. It would not affect, in the slightest degree, any of the laws referred to, except it would take away the power from any one person to compel another person whom he had promised to pay actual money to take promises instead.

Mr. BECK. You mean that would be the result if the legal-tender clause were taken away in some other form; but if the resolution becomes a law, the effect I have stated would be produced?

Secretary SHERMAN. I do not want to criticise the resolution, and I hardly think it proper for you to ask me to do so.

The CHAIRMAN. If it does not take away the legal-tender character of the notes it fails of its intention.

Mr. BECK. You agree, then, that that is a fact; and, agreeing that it is a fact, I desire you to read section 5182, from the word "and," and say whether all bank notes, even after this resolution passes, will not remain a legal tender to banks, to creditors of the government, to members of Congress, and to everybody else?

The CHAIRMAN. To creditors of the government—all of them?

Mr. BECK. Yes, sir; all but the bondholders.

Mr. ALLISON. There is no doubt about that.

Mr. BECK. What I want to show is that this resolution destroys everything but the bank notes, and that all their power remains.

Mr. KERNAN. Do you understand that if this resolution passes national-bank notes would still be a legal tender?

Mr. BECK. I do.

Secretary SHERMAN. The national-bank law clearly provides that the bank notes shall be received at par by the United States itself, and shall be paid out for all salaries or other debts and demands owing by the United States to individuals, except interest on the public debt, and in redemption of national currency—the same provision applies to United States notes—and also the additional quality of being an enforced legal tender between private parties in payment of private contracts. Now, as a matter of course, you ask me an ungracious question when you desire my comments upon a bill introduced by a member of the Senate, also chairman of this committee, and I do not wish to express any opinion, because that is a matter of construction.

Mr. BECK. The Senator who introduced the resolution himself says that if that resolution passes as it stands and becomes a law, the effect I have stated will be produced.

Secretary SHERMAN. I would rather let the Senator give his own opinion about that.

Mr. BECK. I understood him to say that to you a little while ago. Assuming that that is the fact, would not the bank notes still remain a legal tender under that section of the law I have just read to you both from the government and the banks?

Secretary SHERMAN. There is no doubt about the law, so far as the bank note is concerned, that it is payable for all salaries and receivable for all dues to the United States except the exempted ones.

Mr. BECK. And the passage of the resolution I have just read would not affect that law as to national-bank notes in any form?

Secretary SHERMAN. Now, I must decline to give my opinion as to the meaning of the bill—it puts me in a delicate position; but if you ask my opinion of what ought to be done——

Mr. BECK. I am asking you about the pending resolution. Would there be any paper money left after that resolution was passed that the government could require any person to take except the national-bank notes, and would not the national-bank notes remain after that resolution with all the powers they now have, and with all the rights of the government to require persons to take them; would not that be the construction of the Treasury Department?

Secretary SHERMAN. I think you had better leave that to others, because the language is plain enough. My opinion is that United States notes ought to have all the sanction that the government can possibly give to them, to be receivable and payable for all purposes that the government can clearly make them receivable or make them payable for; and that we ought to attempt to make a contract between individuals payable in United States notes when, by the general principle of law, it is payable in standard money and not in promises.

Mr. BECK. Is it your opinion that it would be good policy to allow the national-bank notes to continue in existence with a greater paying power than United States notes?

Secretary SHERMAN. No, sir. I would give to the United States notes every sanction and use that could possibly be given to them without invading and trenching upon a power which it is very doubtful if Congress possesses; that is, the power to make money out of a promise to pay money. The Parliament of England does not assume such a power as this for itself; and in granting authority to the Bank of England to issue notes it specially provides that the notes shall be a legal tender only as long as they are actually redeemed in coin, as will be seen by the following act.

AN ACT for giving to the corporation of the Governor and Company of the Bank of England certain privileges for a limited period, under certain conditions, approved August 29, 1833.

SEC. 6. *And be it further enacted,* That from and after the 1st day of August, 1834, unless and until Parliament shall otherwise direct, a tender of a note or notes of the Governor and Company of the Bank of England, expressed to be payable to bearer on demand, shall be a legal tender to the amount expressed in such note or notes, and shall be taken to be valid as a tender to such amount for all sums above £5 on all occasions on which any tender of money may be legally made, *so long as the Bank of England shall continue to pay on demand their said notes in legal coin.*

Mr. BECK. You are very clear in giving us your opinion that any law or resolution that would leave the national-bank note with a higher paying power or a greater capacity for usefulness than a United States note would not be good policy.

Secretary SHERMAN. I think so.

Mr. BECK. These laws that I have read to you you say you do not care to construe particularly.

Secretary SHERMAN. I am willing to construe the law, but I do not wish to construe the meaning of a bill proposed by a Senator, and that Senator a member of this committee.

Mr. BECK. Then will you be kind enough to construe the law set forth in section 5182 of the Revised Statutes?

Secretary SHERMAN. I say that under that section 5182 the bank bills would be receivable at par for all dues to the United States except duties on imports, and that they would also be legally payable for all salaries and other debts and demands owing by the United States to individuals.

Mr. BECK. Now turn to another section 5196, on a succeeding page, and say as to the power contained in that. Would not each national bank in the United States be required to take the notes of every other national bank in payment of all debts due to the bank?

Secretary SHERMAN. "Every national-banking association formed or existing under this title shall take and receive at par, for any debt or liability to it, any and all notes or bills issued by any lawfully organized national-banking association. But this provision shall not apply to any association organized for the purpose of issuing notes payable in gold."

Mr. BECK. So that power would still remain should this resolution become a law?

The CHAIRMAN. This resolution has no reference whatever to bank notes, it has no effect upon them one way or another, and was not intended to have.

Mr. BECK. Would not the bank notes then continue to have this additional use, supposing the resolution to become a law?

Secretary SHERMAN. That is another form of asking me to construe a bill. I am willing to give you my construction of the law. I have already stated that I do not think any quality should be given to a bank note that is not given to United States notes as long as the latter exist.

Mr. BECK. If a law is passed depriving the United States notes of all legal-tender quality in the payment of debt from the United States to the individual or from banks or individuals, and the present United States banking laws remain as they are, will not the notes of the banks have a much higher quality than United States notes thus deprived of the power that they formerly had?

Secretary SHERMAN. I should say not.

Mr. BECK. I am speaking as if that resolution should pass and become a law.

Secretary SHERMAN. You ask me this question provided that became a law?

Mr. BECK. Should that become a law?

Secretary SHERMAN. That is the same thing over again. I do not think, Mr. Senator, you ought to ask me that question, because that is a matter you are called upon to decide and pass upon in your sphere as a Senator. I would say, on the other hand, that I do not think it ought to have any such effect. I suppose, however, Mr. Bayard would very frankly tell you what the intention of the resolution is.

The CHAIRMAN. I know one thing: That banks can not compel me to receive their notes for debts due me, nor can any man compel me to receive them. If the government owes me my salary, I think they could, perhaps, pay me in the national-bank notes under the existing law, but you cannot compel the payment of a debt between private parties with it.

Secretary SHERMAN. If you will allow me, I should like to amplify a little on one point: I think if Congress would take up this question of the modification of the legal-tender note and make certain rules of evidence (which would be clearly constitutional), which good lawyers undoubtedly approve, declaring that where a contract is made between parties upon the basis of United States notes, it shall be presumed by courts in the affirmance of contracts that the payment in United States notes shall be a sufficient compliance therewith, and that, in the absence of any absolute provision to the contrary, paper money, or promises to pay money, shall be a legal tender in discharge of any obligation. The United States in repealing the legal-tender quality, which is a question for Congress, may by declaratory law easily avoid the constitutional difficulty, so that no one's rights would be disturbed. Now, the only objection I ever heard to the repeal of the legal-tender clause is that some unreasonable creditor might, in order to oppress a debtor without notice, demand coin. The answer to that is that it probably would never be done. Of course a man might do it and demand coin in this way, thus putting the debtor to inconvenience.

The CHAIRMAN. Putting the creditor to inconvenience! Was there ever a period in our history when the creditor was put to so little inconvenience? Was there ever so much money and was it ever so cheap?

Secretary SHERMAN. I have in the past collected much money for my clients, and I never knew such a demand as I have referred to, to be made; but still it might be made.

Mr. BECK. Suppose I contract with a party for the purchase of certain things, the condition being payment on a certain day in money; and suppose on that day I tender United States notes and he refuses them and demands coin?

Secretary SHERMAN. Suppose the coin is demanded? How easy, if necessary, to send to New York and get it.

Mr. BECK. But you are to pay on a given day, and without a minute's warning.

The CHAIRMAN. There never was a time when such a demand could be so readily met.

Mr. MORRILL. If a man makes a tender and it is not objected to——

Mr. KERNAN. But if he should object or demand payment in coin it becomes necessary for him to give me a reasonable time to comply with the demand.

Mr. FERRY. Would it be well to fix the rights of communities upon a basis of prosperity?

The CHAIRMAN. That is the time of all times to fix it, because there can be hardship to no man then. If you should fix it in a time of great distress you would undoubtedly create a great deal of hardship; and it is to avoid that and to enact some law which will prevent the possibility of depreciation of money that this resolution is offered.

Mr. FERRY. You are limiting the rights of individuals under a prosperous condition.

The CHAIRMAN. And it is to prevent any possibility of injury to the interests of men that this measure should be adopted now at a time when nobody will suffer, and affairs will settle themselves.

Mr. FERRY. If you fix a man's rights on a basis of resumption, when a time comes that resumption fails his rights are injured.

The CHAIRMAN. The very object of the measure is to prevent that result in the future. It cannot hurt a man to-day who is called upon to pay in coin, because he can get it on demand.

Mr. WALLACE. Allow me to ask you whether, under the act of 1864, United States notes being a lawful money, and the owners of the capital stock of these national banking associations having invested their money upon the faith of the law as it then stood, it did not become a contract under which if we now take away the power of legal tender from the lawful money then in existence, they still have the right to pay their outstanding notes with United States Treasury notes, notwithstanding the lawful tender is taken away from them ?

Secretary SHERMAN. My impression is that if you simply take away the legal-tender quality of United States notes you still have in full force the provision of the bank note, because the United States notes are still considered as lawful money, just as the fractional coin is lawful money, though it is not a legal tender for more than ten dollars.

Mr. WALLACE. The effect, then, of taking away the legal-tender quality from United States notes would extend simply to contracts between private parties, and could not affect the provisions of the bank charters ?

Secretary SHERMAN. I think not, because the national banking law expressly provides that the banks shall have the privilege of redeeming their notes in United States notes or coin.

Mr. WALLACE. In the "lawful money" of the United States (reading the words of the section). Your opinion is that that continues lawful money until the charter of the bank expires ?

Secretary SHERMAN. Yes, sir; that is it. If you simply say, "I pay you $500," that means coin dollars; but if you say, "I pay you in lawful money $500, or currency, or United States notes, or bank notes," then it would be enforced as a stipulation. In the absence, however, of express stipulation, it means naked money.

Mr. KERNAN. Under the bank charters these banks have a right to redeem in whatever was lawful money at the time of the granting of the charter.

Mr. WALLACE. The Secretary has answered that.

Secretary SHERMAN. I think you have a right to change it, but I do not think the passage of the resolution would do it.

Mr. ALLISON. Do you think we do not do it by that language when we say, "and shall not be otherwise a legal tender "?

Secretary SHERMAN. I do not say what the construction is. I say if you take away the legal-tender quality from United States notes, and nothing else, you will still have, under the provisions creating them lawful money, a right to treat them as lawful money, and to issue an execution payable in lawful money, or United States notes, because there is no provision in this resolution that says United States notes shall not be lawful money.

Mr. WALLACE. Is it not your opinion that the national banks could redeem their notes in United States Treasury notes if the legal-tender quality were taken away ?

Secretary SHERMAN. Undoubtedly so.

Mr. WALLACE. And because of the fact that United States notes are lawful money, and the words " lawful money " entered into the construction of the banking charters ?

Secretary SHERMAN. The law still says they may be redeemed in lawful money.

Mr. FERRY. If the legal-tender quality were removed, would not there be this condition of things : Suppose in receiving the proceeds of a discounted note from a national bank I take from the bank United States notes——

Secretary SHERMAN. You would not then be bound to take that currency.

Mr. FERRY. But I do take it, and at the maturity of the note I go to the bank to take the note up with the United States notes from which the legal-tender feature has been taken away, and the bank refuse to take them ?

Secretary SHERMAN. The banks are bound to take United States notes and notes of other national banks.

Mr. FERRY. Can I compel the bank to take them with this provision in the law ?

Secretary SHERMAN. Yes, sir.

Mr. FERRY. With the legal-tender feature removed from the United States notes ?

Secretary SHERMAN. O, yes; they are bound to take them.

Mr. FERRY. Under what clause of the law ?

Secretary SHERMAN. I cannot turn to it now.

Mr. ALLISON. I have before me your report of December last. It contains your views and judgment of what we ought to do in regard to the repeal of the legal-tender clause ?

Secretary SHERMAN. Yes, sir.

Mr. ALLISON. You have not changed your views since that report was submitted.

Secretary SHERMAN. No, sir; not in regard to that. I ought to say that I think my views are sufficiently stated in that report.

Mr. ALLISON. You say, "the Secretary therefore respectfully submits to Congress whether the legal-tender clause should not now be repealed as to all future contracts." Do I understand that to be your recommendation with reference to what we ought to do ?

Secretary SHERMAN. Yes ; but that is for Congress to determine. I think it is well enough to reserve prior contracts ; for I do not think we ought or want to do anything to violate existing contracts.

Mr. ALLISON. Is that your recommendation ?

Secretary SHERMAN. Yes, sir; that is my recommendation.

Mr. ALLISON. That whatever we do in reference to this clause should apply to future contracts ?

Secretary SHERMAN. Yes, sir.

Mr. ALLISON. And not to any existing contracts ?

Secretary SHERMAN. I think so.

Mr. ALLISON. Is not that individual opinion of yours based upon the idea that we, having issued these notes to public creditors—for they are nothing but debts of the United States—and having given to our creditors who hold these notes the option to use them in payment of debts, that as long as those particular notes are outstanding they ought to be used in payment of debts now existing.

Secretary SHERMAN. I think that is a reservation that it is always safe to make where you change the form of payment—a reservation as to existing contracts.

Mr. ALLISON. These notes on their face say they are a legal tender for private debts. Now, do you not regard that obligation as sacred as the obligation which you are seeking to protect?

Secretary SHERMAN. No; I think the public faith and the public credit is fully supported when we are ready to redeem these notes in coin.

Mr. ALLISON. That is true while we redeem them in coin; but you said awhile ago that you were not quite willing to have this provision in regard to payment of customs dues in notes made absolute now, because there might come a time when we could not redeem them in coin. Now, I hold one of these United States notes; it is to me a debt-paying power. Of course, while you are redeeming these notes in coin there is no practical difference between the notes and coin; but suppose you cease to redeem them in coin; suppose a contingency which you presumed would not happen in reference to the interest on the public debt should happen with reference to these notes, would it be a good thing—supposing that contingency—to take away by law a power that these notes in my possession now have? Would it not be a violation of the public faith, as much as a violation which might be implied by a repeal or abrogation of the provision of the act of 1862?

Secretary SHERMAN. I see no analogy between the two. In the first place, here is a stipulation, on behalf of an indebtedness that is running by express terms for 30 years, that you will set aside a specific fund for its payment; while on the other hand the note is payable now. Suppose we say we are ready to pay off these notes that are in the holder's hands; can he have any right to complain? Suppose we say, "If you do not present that note within five years we will not pay it at all." A statute of limitation is within the power of Congress, and is a matter of wise discretion.

Mr. ALLISON. Here is a note that on its face says it is a legal tender for $5. We are redeeming these notes in coin to-day. Suppose to-morrow we lack the ability to redeem this note in coin, it still remaining in the hands of a public creditor—because I am a public creditor, and the government owes me that amount; now, is there not a shade of violation of public faith in saying that, although I hold that note in my possession, having that legal-tender quality impressed upon it, that quality shall be taken away by law without payment of that note?

Secretary SHERMAN. I do not think there is any analogy. We are ready to pay it now. That is simply a promise to pay so much money; and, as I have suggested, we give you notice if you do not present it within a given time we will not pay it.

Mr. ALLISON. So we are ready as regards the payment of customs dues to enact that they shall be paid in United States notes; but you say, and I agree with you, that it it is not fair to violate, even in spirit, that law of 1862. Is it any more fair to violate, that law which says that the note in my hand is a legal tender?

Secretary SHERMAN. I do not see any analogy.

Mr. FERRY. To-day, Mr. Secretary, under resumption, you are ready to pay that note in coin; to-morrow you cease paying and cease resumption, on account of the condition of the country. That note is good to a party for $5. in payment to any one he owes, and you propose to take that power away from it. You say you are ready to pay it, and he presents it after you have ceased to resume, and you do not pay it in coin, while you have taken away the power which this note had of liquidating $5 of debt for every individual. Now, is not that a violation of faith?

3 SH

Secretary SHERMAN. It would be a violation of public credit and faith to refuse to redeem our United States notes after the resumption act had gone into operation, and I do not wish to admit that we will do that.

Mr. FERRY. You said there might be a condition of war, when you might be no longer ready to redeem. I cite that condition, and you say you are unable to pay that note, but you still propose to take away the legal-tender feature of it, and to take away the power it has of paying debt.

Mr. ALLISON. The act of June 20, 1874, provides in specific terms that when national-bank notes are presented at the Treasury for redemption, you can redeem them in United States notes.

Secretary SHERMAN. Yes, sir.

Mr. ALLISON. It provides that such association shall, upon notification, deposit United States notes equal to the amount of its notes so redeemed.

Secretary SHERMAN. We do that every day unless we can get them to take coin.

Mr. ALLISON. But would you consider it, after the passage of this law—I am sorry you cannot construe that law which provides that each bank shall keep a deposit in the Treasury of the United States in lawful money of the United States—a compliance with this law for a national bank to send you United States notes?

Secretary SHERMAN. I do not see anything in this law, and I do not think there is anything in the bill, that would prevent it from being considered as lawful money; but I say I do not propose myself, and I do not think there is anything in Senator Bayard's bill, that would change that feature.

The CHAIRMAN. That is a question of construction. I have never questioned the power of the government to emit bills of credit, but I claim that those bills of credit cannot be made money when they are but the evidence of money borrowed.

Mr. ALLISON. I want to get at the operation of this banking law if you should pass the pending resolution. Now, the law provides that national banks shall redeem their notes at the Treasury, and in order to do that they "shall keep and have on deposit in the Treasury of the United States, in lawful money of the United States, a sum equal to five per centum of its circulation"; would you understand it to be a sufficient compliance with this law to deposit United States notes to the extent of five per cent. after the passage of this law?

Secretary SHERMAN. I do not construe this proposed law, but after the repeal of the legal-tender clause these notes would still be lawful money—lawfully issued and called money; but a promise to pay that money as between private parties the courts would undoubtedly require to be in specific terms. I do not want to enter into the controversy whether a United States note deprived of this legal-tender quality is what is called lawful money. It is claimed that unless you repeal that provision which makes it lawful money it still continues to be such.

Mr. ALLISON. As I understand you, then, without construing Mr. Bayard's proposed law, in any arrangement you would still provide that these United States notes might be deposited by national banks, and that the government might redeem the bank notes in United States notes?

Secretary SHERMAN. I would not say anything about that; that is a grave question. After the repeal of the legal-tender clause the notes would, as I understand it, still stand as lawful money, and wherever in a contract lawful money is prescribed they would be considered lawful money—that is, money lawfully issued.

Mr. ALLISON. This would be a very grave question, as you see, as to what could be done with bank notes. We have provided a mode of redeeming them. Would a deposit by a bank of United States notes be a substantial compliance with the law, or ought it to be considered a substantial compliance?

Secretary SHERMAN. I think so.

Mr. ALLISON. Then of course the government, if that is a substantial compliance, would redeem its promises by also paying out United States notes?

Secretary SHERMAN. I think so. I think that under the law United States notes ought to be received and paid out precisely as they are now. No difference in that regard should be made except that the United States should not attempt to make these promises to pay, actual money as between private parties.

Mr. FERRY. Then they would be simply lawful paper instead of lawful money?

Secretary SHERMAN. They would be lawful money.

Mr. BECK. In the act of June 20, 1874, when speaking of the five per cent. that shall be held in the Treasury for redemption, this language is used:

That every association * * * shall at all times keep and have on deposit in the Treasury of the United States, in the lawful money of the United States, a sum equal to five per centum of its circulation, to be held and used for the redemption of such circulation.

You think you would still have the right under that law to do that after the legal-tender clause was taken away?

Secretary SHERMAN. Undoubtedly they would still be United States notes.

Mr. BECK. I ask you, then, if when these notes are so deposited the United States has any power to pay them out; and, I speak of *power*, how can they ever be reissued again under the law of May, 1868, if the United States has no power to make them a legal tender for anything?

Secretary SHERMAN. But they can be reissued. We could say what we would receive them for, and we could pay our public officers with them as before stated. That is the law now.

Mr. BECK. Suppose we pass a law——

Secretary SHERMAN. You do not want me to construe that.

Mr. BECK. Suppose we had passed a law saying that they shall not be otherwise legal tender, would we have any power to reissue them?

Secretary SHERMAN. I do not desire to construe a pending measure.

Mr. BECK. As soon as we destroy the legal-tender quality can we do any more than receive them at the Treasury? Suppose I had $10,000 of them on the day before the passage of the act, and I have made a contract to buy my neighbor's farm and to pay him on a certain day in legal-tender notes as I have a right, and I take them to him on that day after the passage of the act when they are no longer a legal tender?

Secretary SHERMAN. The contract having been made?

Mr. BECK. The contract having been made and the medium of payment fixed, would you regard it as a matter of good faith on the part of the government to thus put me in a condition where I would be at the mercy of the other party?

Secretary SHERMAN. If the contract had been made before the passage of the act, then the act should not apply, for I would not recommend the passage of any act which applied to pre existing contracts.

The CHAIRMAN. Would you not give him an equivalent for gold or silver if you offered to pay him in the notes?

Secretary SHERMAN. If the tender was made and declined, the courts have held over and over again that a reasonable time is to be allowed for the party to get the coin, and the courts have also held that a mere refusal to accept current money as a legal tender should not be made the means of depriving a man of his rights under the contract, if in a reasonable time he complies with it.

Mr. BECK. Would that hold where the contract was specific as to the time and the medium of payment.

The CHAIRMAN. That would be rather a difficult question for the court to decide.

Mr. ALLISON. In my State we make time the essence of the agreement, and if the contract is to do a certain thing on a certain day I must do it on that day.

The CHAIRMAN. There is no escaping the fact that there never was a time since this was a government when it was so easy to pay in specie as it is to-day.

Mr. ALLISON. That is the truth, and it is a fact.

The CHAIRMAN. The methods of adjusting balances were never so perfect; there never was by one-half as large a volume of silver and gold in the country as to-day, and therefore every one of these objections based upon the inability to pay in coin was never so improbable as now.

Mr. ALLISON. Laws are made for changing conditions.

The CHAIRMAN. I know they are, and that is the reason why we should take the present time in which to change this law.

The next subject is—

COST OF REFUNDING.

The CHAIRMAN. "What has been the cost of converting the interest-bearing debt, as it stood July 14, 1870, to what it is now, including double interest, commissions, traveling expenses of agents, &c., and the use of public money by banks, and the value of its use, so as to determine whether the system should be continued or changed?"

Mr. BECK. I would say to the Secretary, if you will allow me now, that I may desire, after looking over the statement that he makes, to ask some questions which I am not quite prepared to ask now.

Secretary SHERMAN. I would rather give you these official statements and let you look them over for yourself, and ask me such questions as you may think necessary.

Referring to the expenses for refunding, the law appropriated one-half of one per cent. to cover all forms of expenditure. Under the refunding operations $500,000,000 of five per cent. bonds were sold by my predecessors, in which they contracted to pay to the syndicate or other parties who sold the bonds one-half of one per cent., the contracting parties to pay all the expenses of the loan out of that commission. The result was that on the $500,000,000 of five per cent. bonds the amount paid for expenses was $2,500,000.

Mr. BECK. That was under whose administration?

Secretary SHERMAN. That was under the administration of Secretaries Boutwell, Richardson, and Bristow, and the same provision existed in the contract made by Secretary Morrill for the sale of $300,000,000

4½ per cents; which contract was in force when I took charge of the Treasury.

Mr. BECK. That was the contract in relation to four-and-a half per cents?

Secretary SHERMAN. Yes, sir; he allowed the syndicate one-half of one per cent., they to pay all the expenses. including hire of clerical force and incidental expenses of every kind. The amount of bonds placed under that contract for refunding was $185,000,000, on which the commission amounted to $925,000.

When I assumed the office of Secretary of the Treasury, and after this contract was closed, I adopted a different policy. In selling four per cent. bonds I assumed the payment of all expenses. I thought that the transactions being so large I could save something out of the one-half per cent. allowed by law, and I did in the summer of 1877, in selling the four per cent. bonds, save something, although not much. After that, when the syndicates were abandoned—the public at large do not seem to know that after 1877 there were no syndicates at all, except for resumption purposes and the foreign contract of January, 1872—all bonds were sold upon public advertisements, copies of which I have here. We sold $740,845,950, including the bonds sold for resumption purposes, and the whole expense of placing that amount to date is $2,591,922.26. The one-half per cent. provided for by law amounted to $3,704,229.75. thus leaving a balance unexpended of the one-half per cent. commission of $1,112,307.49.

Mr. ALLISON. You say that after 1877 there were no syndicates?

Secretary SHERMAN. No syndicates except for the loan sold in Europe and for resumption purposes.

Mr. ALLISON. And most of this $700,000,000 of four per cents which were placed was without the intervention of the syndicate?

Secretary SHERMAN. All except about $15,000,000, which were sold abroad in London ; and I have brought two circulars here under which this was done. This method was adopted, as the correspondence shows, only after careful consideration, and some serious doubts as to whether we could manage the machinery of the national banks to do it without the aid of a syndicate; but I ventured to try it on the 16th January, 1878. Here is the first circular issued by me after the syndicate contracts ended :

TREASURY DEPARTMENT,
Washington, D. C., January 16, 1878.

The Secretary of the Treasury hereby gives notice that, from the 26th instant, and until further notice, he will receive subscriptions for the four per cent. funded loan of the United States, in denominations as stated below, at par and accrued interest, in coin.

The bonds are redeemable July 1, 1907. and bear interest, payable quarterly, on the first day of January, April, July, and October of each year, and are exempt from the payment of taxes or duties to the United States, as well as from taxation in any form by or under State, municipal, or local authority.

The subscriptions may be made for coupon bonds of $50, $100, $500, and $1,000, and for registered bonds of $50, $100, $500, $1,000, $5,000, and $10,000.

Two per cent. of the purchase money must accompany the subscription; the remainder may be paid at the pleasure of the purchaser, either at time of subscription or within thirty days thereafter, with interest on the amount of the subscription, at the rate of four per cent. per annum, to date of payment.

Upon the receipt of full payment, the bonds will be transmitted, free of charge to the subscribers, and a commission of one-fourth of one per cent. will be allowed upon the amount of subscriptions, but no commission will be paid upon any single subscription less than $1,000.

Forms of application will be furnished by the Treasurer at Washington, the assistant treasurers at Baltimore, Boston, Chicago, Cincinnati, New Orleans, New York, Philadelphia, Saint Louis, and San Francisco, and by the national banks and bankers generally. The applications must specify the amount and denominations required, and, for registered bonds, the full name and post-office address of the person to whom the bonds shall be made payable.

The interest on the registered bonds will be paid by check, issued by the Treasurer of the United States, to the order of the holder, and mailed to his address. The check is payable on presentation, properly indorsed, at the office of the Treasurer and assistant treasurers of the United States.

Payments for the bonds may be made in coin to the Treasurer of the United States at Washington, or assistant treasurers at Baltimore, Boston, Chicago, Cincinnati, New Orleans, New York, Philadelphia, Saint Louis, and San Francisco.

To promote the convenience of subscribers, the department will also receive, in lieu of coin, called bonds of the United States, coupons past due or maturing within thirty days, or gold certificates issued under the act of March 3, 1863, and national banks will be designated as depositaries under the provisions of section 5153, Revised Statutes of the United States, to receive deposits on account of this loan, under regulations to be hereafter prescribed.

JOHN SHERMAN,
Secretary of the Treasury.

That circular proposed that all the banks should become public depositaries; and under its provisions, 148 of them (which is but a small portion of the number of banks, there being over 2,000) came into the scheme from time to time, although all were invited and were offered the same commission of one-fourth of one per cent. upon the amount subscribed, no commission, however, to be paid on a subscription of less than $1,000. That proposition continued during that year, and under it we sold about $125,000,000.

The CHAIRMAN. Did that one-fourth per cent. include the expenses?

Secretary SHERMAN. No; we paid the expenses ourselves, and we allowed subscribers a commission of one-fourth per cent., paying the expenses out of the remaining quarter and thus saving considerable.

We did not change that order, I think, in any particular.

The CHAIRMAN. What portion of that remaining quarter per cent. did you expend in expenses?

Secretary SHERMAN. As nearly as I can tell, about one-half during the first of that year.

The CHAIRMAN. That made the total expense ⅜ per cent.?

Secretary SHERMAN. Three-eighths per cent. But after that we saved a good deal more because we reduced the commission.

And then on January 1, 1879, I issued another circular, of which this is a copy:

1879.
Department No. 3.
Secretary's office.

TREASURY DEPARTMENT,
SECRETARY'S OFFICE,
Washington, D. C., January 1, 1879.

The Secretary of the Treasury calls attention to the four per cent. funded Loan of the United States now offered by this department in denominations, viz: for coupon bonds of $50, $100, $500, and $1,000, and for registered bonds of $50, $100, $500, $1,000, $5,000, and $10,000, at par and accrued interest to date of subscription, in coin.

The bonds are redeemable July 1, 1907, and bear interest, payable quarterly, on the first day of January, April, July, and October of each year, and are exempt from the payment of taxes or duties to the United States, as well as from taxation in any form by or under State, municipal, or local authority.

Upon the receipt of full payment, the bonds will be transmitted, free of charge, to the subscribers.

Applications should specify the amount and denominations required, and, for registered bonds, the full name and post-office address of the person to whom the bonds shall be made payable.

The interest on the registered bonds will be paid by check, issued by the Treasurer of the United States, to the order of the holder, and mailed to his address. The check is payable on presentation, properly indorsed, at the office of the assistant treasurer of the United States in New York, in coin or United States notes, as the holder may prefer, or, if desired, in United States notes at the office of the Treasurer or any assistant treasurer of the United States.

All national banks are again invited to become financial agents of the government and depositaries of public moneys received on the sale of these bonds, upon complying with Section 5153, Revised Statutes of the United States. All banks, bankers, post-masters, and other public officers, and all other persons, are invited to aid in placing these bonds. They can make their arrangements through national banks for the deposit of the purchase-money of the bonds.

The money received by depository banks on account of subscriptions will remain on deposit with said banks, but subject to the order of the Treasurer of the United States, and calls for the redemption of six per cent. bonds will issue from time to time as the Secretary may direct.

Payments may be made to the Treasurer of the United States at Washington, or assistant treasurers at Baltimore, Boston, Chicago, Cincinnati, New Orleans, New York, Philadelphia, Saint Louis, and San Francisco, in coin, matured coupons, coin certificates, or United States notes.

The Secretary of the Treasury will also accept in payment called bonds, certificates of deposit of national banks specially designated to receive deposits on this account, but the bonds will not be delivered until the certificate has been paid for by a Treasury draft, or by a deposit of a like amount of coin with the Treasurer or some assistant treasurer of the United States, or until other United States bonds of equal amount are substituted in their stead.

The Treasurer of the United States will also accept, in payment, United States coupons maturing within thirty days, or drafts in favor of himself drawn on New York, which will be collected and the excess, if any, returned by check to the depositor.

Commissions will be allowed on subscriptions for said bonds only, as follows:

On an aggregate of subscriptions of $100,000, and not exceeding $1,000,000, between January 1, 1879, and June 30, 1879, one-eighth of one per cent. On an aggregate of subscriptions exceeding $1,000,000, and not exceeding $10,000,000, between the same dates, one-quarter of one per cent., and on amounts in excess of $10,000,000 an additional commission of one-tenth of one per cent.

All blanks, or forms, or information needed, will be furnished by the department without cost.

This circular is in lieu of all others previously issued in relation to subscriptions for four per cent. bonds, consols of 1907.

JOHN SHERMAN,
Secretary.

In this I reduced the commission and made it a graded one; one-eighth of one per cent. on all under $1,000,000, and one-fourth of one per cent. on all over $1,000,000 and not exceeding $10,000,000, with an additional one-tenth of one per cent. for all over $10,000,000. My object was to get strong competition between the great banks that were then competing, but finding it did not work very well, and there was complaint made by banks, I soon changed that by allowing a commission of one-eighth all around, and under that circular the great saving was made. We saved of course under the other, because a large portion of the subscriptions were taken for one eighth commission, and some for one-fourth.

The commissions that were paid have all been reported to Congress, and printed in a public document in reply to a resolution of Mr. Saulsbury. (Senate Doc. No. 9, 1st session 46th Cong.) The amount paid to every person is published, except those that have been paid since that publication, which latter payments are contained in the paper you have before you, giving the commissions paid to each person. (House Ex. Doc. No. 9, 2nd session 46th Congress.)

A great deal of criticism has been made in the public press, and I think you have referred to it in your speech [addressing Mr. Beck], about the commissions earned, or the large profits made by the First National Bank of New York. I desire to say here that no favor of any kind was ever granted to that bank or any other bank, so far as I know, and I have had the whole matter searched from beginning to end.

The First National had no account with us, except the same that all other depositary banks have. We never deposited any money with it, and these banks engaged in the refunding operations, were not depositaries in the sense of having money placed in their hands by the government. The whole deposits with them were on account of sales, that they or anybody through them made, because thousands of people did business through them. They were to send us a certificate of these deposits which would be secured by bonds through the Treasurer, and then at the end of the ninety days we would call the money in for the payment of called bonds. The money was left there for ninety days, and through those transactions enormous sums appear, represented by their certificates, and by actual bonds deposited with the assistant treasurer in New York.

The CHAIRMAN. These bonds were deposited as security?

Secretary SHERMAN. Deposited as security.

The CHAIRMAN. They were their own bonds?

Secretary SHERMAN. They were government bonds.

The CHAIRMAN. But they owned the government bonds?

Secretary SHERMAN. Yes, sir; they or their correspondents.

Mr. BECK. And were drawing the interest upon them all the time, of course?

Secretary SHERMAN. Here is a table showing the sales and commissions of certain banks. I have taken all banks who sold over $1,000,000. There were twenty-six of them. This First National Bank, having been always connected with the national securities and having been the agent of the syndicate, continued to be the agent of the foreign syndicate, and continued to have altogether the largest business. They sold of the four per cent. bonds $262,625,000. The sales of the other banks are kept here in the same way. The Bank of New York (National Banking Association), I think, was the next. It sold $57,259,500. The National Bank of Commerce sold $51,684,000; the National Bank of the State of New York sold $46,915,000, and so on down.

Subscriptions of and commissions paid to national banks on account of the four per cent. loan, whose sales were $1,000,001 or more.

No.	Banks.	Sales in 1878.	Sales in 1879; circular of Jan. 1.	Sales under circular April 16, '79.	Total.	Amount of commission paid.
1	First National Bank of New York	$54,125,000	$87,500,000	$121,000,000	$362,625,000	$362,812 50
2	Chase National Bank of New York	1,846,350	1,626,100	500,000	3,972,450	9,306 12
3	Bank of New York (National Banking Association)	10,136,000	34,143,500	12,500,000	57,259,500	134,792 25
4	National Bank of the State of New York	7,770,000	27,145,000	12,000,000	46,915,000	104,432 50
5	Second National Bank of New York	1,500,000	2,200,050		3,700,000	9,250 00
6	Hanover National Bank of New York		17,995,300		17,995,300	52,993 55
7	Continental National Bank of New York		34,697,550		36,697,550	113,911 42
8	Chemical National Bank of New York		3,200,200	2,000,000	3,200,000	8,000 50
9	National Broadway Bank of New York		1,200,000		1,200,000	3,000 00
10	National Albany Exchange Bank of Albany, New York	1,325,000	1,531,400		2,856,400	7,141 00
11	Maverick National Bank of Boston, Massachusetts	10,250,000	25,000,000		35,250,000	103,125 00
12	Monument National Bank of Charlestown, Massachusetts	1,880,000	7,520,000		9,400,000	23,500 00
13	Pacific National Bank of Boston, Massachusetts	530,800	1,000,000		1,530,800	3,837 00
14	Manufacturers' National Bank of Boston, Massachusetts	325,000	555,000		1,100,000	1,841 25
15	National Security Bank of Boston, Massachusetts	1,625,000	1,100,000		2,725,000	6,812 50
16	National Bank of the Commonwealth, Boston, Massachusetts	500,000	500,000		1,300,000	2,250 00
17	First National Bank of Chelsea, Massachusetts	87,050	103,050		190,700	2,976 73
18	City National Bank of Plainfield, New Jersey	290,000	712,000		1,002,000	1,615 00
19	Tradesmen's National Bank of Pittsburgh, Pennsylvania	282,750	918,550		1,201,300	3,003 25
20	Wachusett National Bank of Fitchburg, Massachusetts	1,150,000	1,002,700		2,152,700	5,381 75
21	Franklin County National Bank of Greenfield, Massachusetts	10,000	1,002,200		1,012,200	2,530 50
22	First National Bank of Cincinnati, Ohio	430,000	1,050,000		1,480,000	3,700 00
23	Third National Bank of Cincinnati, Ohio		1,000,000	1,000,000	2,000,000	3,750 00
24	Fourth National Bank of Cincinnati, Ohio		2,000,000		2,000,000	5,000 00
25	First National Bank of Newburyport, Massachusetts	396,500	1,062,500		1,399,000	3,497 50
26	National Bank of Commerce of New York	6,331,000	45,350,000		51,664,000	161,560 00
	Total	100,773,450	302,655,650	149,000,000	552,929,100	1,363,070 34

At one time there was a great competition between these large banks for the additional commission. When a bank fell a little short of subscribing the $10,000,000, it complained bitterly of not getting the extra commission, and these complaints caused me to make a uniform commission of one-fourth per cent.

The total amount sold to the above banks was $552,929,100, and the amount of commissions paid to each as stated in this paper. The commissions paid to the First National Bank were $582,812. The largest subscription made by that bank was made at the end, they getting $121,000,000 of the last sale; but that was through a combination of nearly all the banks and bankers of New York.

Mr. ALLISON. It was made in their name?

Secretary SHERMAN. It was made in their name.

Mr. BECK. I suppose that was the meaning of the entry made on their return of the profit and loss.

Secretary SHERMAN. That, no doubt, was all it meant, but they made a profit besides this commission, because they made a profit on double interest. That, however, was a matter over which we had no control, because every subscriber selected his bank of deposit. I deem it a matter of considerable credit that we saved over one million dollars in the sale of four per cent. bonds.

The CHAIRMAN. What expenses were there besides that one-fourth per cent. commission?

Secretary SHERMAN. The expenses were for printing and engraving, transporting the bonds, clerical hire; but the whole, including the commission, came to less than ⅜ per cent. We had a very large force employed during the busiest portion of the funding operation.

The CHAIRMAN. The commissions were not quite one-fourth per cent. and the other expenses about one-eighth?

Secretary SHERMAN. Yes, sir.

Mr. FERRY. Then you saved about one-eighth per cent?

Secretary SHERMAN. We saved considerably more than one eighth per cent.

Now, in regard to double interest, the best statement made about that that can be made and in the fewest words was by Secretary Boutwell in his report of 1871:

By the act establishing the national-banking system the Secretary of the Treasury was authorized to make the m depositaries of any public money, except receipts from customs, and the act authorizing the refunding of the national debt directed the Secretary of the Treasury to give three months' notice of the payment of any bonds which, in such notice, might be specified and called for payment. In the same act it was provided that the money received for the new bonds should be used only in payment of bonds outstanding, known as five-twenty bonds. The statute proceeded upon the idea that the holders of five-twenty bonds should receive three months' interest upon their bonds after notice should be given by the government.

As this notice could be given safely only upon subscriptions already made or secured, the general necessary result, even in case the money were paid into and held in the Treasury of the United States, would be a loss of interest for three months.

When this report was made to Congress, this committee, of which I was a member, and also the committee of the House more at length, examined into the whole matter.

Mr. BECK. Do you refer to the time when a committee of the House examined Mr. Boutwell and Jay Cooke?

Secretary SHERMAN. Yes; and Mr. Dawes made the report.

Mr. BECK. We have documents touching upon that. We examined Mr. Patterson and William Butler Duncan, and published a report.

Secretary SHERMAN. Yes, sir.

Mr. BECK. As to the length of time?

Secretary SHERMAN. We could see no way to avoid paying that double interest. I was here, and you and Mr. Bayard were here expecting to shorten the call, and as the process of refunding was then very slow, and the people could not tell when their bonds were called, and were not likely to see the notice, it was thought to be pretty hard to shorten it. We did not contemplate then the enormous transactions that were to come in the then future, or we should have shortened the call.

That was the law when I came into the Treasury, and in order to avoid the payment of this double interest I frequently anticipated calls and devised every way I could to avoid its payment. It is utterly impracticable for us to say exactly how much this double interest amounts to. It could not in any case exceed one per cent.

Mr. BECK. O yes.

Secretary SHERMAN. I should say it could not exceed in any case one per cent. on the four per cent. loan. On the five per cent. loan it might be 1¼. Up to the time I came in it was the general rule to exhaust the commission of ½ per cent. allowed by law, and also the ninety days' double interest. Mr. Bristow, however, in a sale of $45,000,000 5 per cent. bonds advanced the price sufficiently to cover the interest, just as I did in selling the 4½ per cents. for resumption purposes, and also in selling the last four per cent. bonds.

As before stated, I adopted the plan of making the calls in advance of subscriptions, and running the risk of selling the new bonds. I would make a call for ten, twenty, or thirty millions in advance of subscriptions. It was a little hazardous, and at the close of the year I was caught with about $15,000,000 ahead of actual sales. But in this way, by calling in advance, we saved, as nearly as we can tell, about one-third of the double interest. Mr. Upton, chief clerk of the Treasury Department, has made a careful estimate, and thinks that it will amount to about three-fourths of one per cent.; but it is practically impossible to state the precise amount.

Mr. ALLISON. Which would make your average call sixty instead of ninety days?

Secretary SHERMAN. Yes. Another thing, when the flood of refunding came, as it did in April, I made a call equal to the whole amount of refunding certificates, in advance, although some of the certificates were not sold until June, and in that way we saved a great deal more; but, as nearly as we can get at it, the amount of double interest paid has been about three fourths of one per cent.

Mr. BECK. There are two matters that I wanted to understand, which, perhaps, you can get at more fully hereafter. First, in what way can we safely change the law as to the length of notice on called bonds. I think the Secretary has once or twice recommended the reduction of the time, and I very much desire to know how far we can pursue the policy in the refunding yet to take place, that he carried out in April with regard to these certificates, so as to make it a more popular loan.

Secretary SHERMAN. Any refunding bill that is passed by Congress ought to make some provision for the issue of these ten dollar certificates. If I had been allowed, under the law, to advance the price of those certificates as I advanced the price of the bonds I could have placed them among the people; but I could not do that; the law expressly authorized that any person by depositing lawful money could obtain these certificates, thus compelling their sale at par. As to the double interest which is to be paid in refunding bonds issued under the refunding act, the refunding act itself requires a notice of ninety days.

Mr. MORRILL. The law under which the five per cents were issued required that before they could be paid off by the process of refunding you must give ninety days' notice.

Mr. ALLISON. That is the law of 1870.

Secretary SHERMAN. Consequently, as to the fives, you cannot make any change in that particular, as that seems to be a part of the contract. We could do it by calling in advance; but that must remain a purely discretionary matter with the Secretary, as you cannot make any rule about it.

Mr. ALLISON. That is, you must issue a call in advance of having the money actually in the Treasury to pay for the bonds?

Secretary SHERMAN. Yes, sir. Suppose you see your sales running along at the rate of twenty or thirty millions a month, you could very easily call the bonds two months in advance. In 1877, by this method of calling in advance, I was twenty millions ahead at one time.

Mr. BECK. The persons who are holding these five per cent. bonds that were issued under the act of 1870 have a right to ninety days' notice.

Secretary SHERMAN. Yes; for all that have been issued under that act. As to the three hundred million of sixes, there is no right of that kind at all, and we can pay them when they are due or at our pleasure. The time fixed for paying them is July, 1881, if we are ready to do so.

You asked about the value of the moneys held at the banks in connection with the refunding operation. That is a matter purely of conjecture. The banks themselves have claimed that the money was not worth to them over two per cent. a year; but that would depend entirely upon the state of the money market. They claimed that they could not use the money to any advantage, because the time they were allowed to retain it was so short. I could not, however, give you any opinion on that, although any banker can tell you about it and about what money was worth to them at that time. It must have been worth a good deal if the report of profits of banks as stated by you is true.

The CHAIRMAN. They might have made those profits by commission.

Mr. MORRILL. They made it on the subsequent rise in bonds.

Mr. BECK. I do not profess to know what their profits were, but they seemed to be very large.

The CHAIRMAN. They were immense; they did not make it out of the government, but out of the people.

Mr. MORRILL. I owned the whole of ten shares in the Maverick National Bank of Boston, and when I was there last fall they were loaded down with five or ten millions of bonds, and were at their wit's end to dispose of them. The bonds were selling some days for one-eighth less than they cost the bank. That is a small bank with a tremendous load of deposits. It has secured the popular reputation of being a well-managed bank, and as a consequence did an immense amount in deposits; but the managers were in great distress to know what to do with those five or ten millions of bonds that they had on their hands, and they were buying as often as selling in order to keep up the price.

SINKING-FUND.

Secretary SHERMAN. I was asked about a sinking-fund, and in reply I will state as follows:

It is the same old question that has been so often debated.

As to the necessity for a sinking-fund and how it is managed, I have only to say that a sinking-fund is nothing more nor less than a name for the surplus revenues of the government, and a government without a surplus revenue cannot possibly have a sinking-fund. There is no way in the world to pay a debt except by having an income above your expenditures, and you can call your surplus revenues a sinking-fund if you choose to do so.

Under existing law the department is required to purchase one per cent. of the entire debt of the United States each fiscal year, and to set the amount apart as a sinking-fund, and to compute interest thereon to be added with the amount to be subsequently purchased each year. This act can only be construed as an authority to purchase the debt in case of surplus revenue for the purpose. Whatever binding force it may have upon Congress to provide revenues sufficient to meet its demands is not for me to say.

There is no particular necessity for this law; any law which provides for and requires the application of surplus revenues to the reduction of the debt would do as well; but if the debt can be decreased at the rate which this act requires, it would be extinguished in about thirty years, and if Congress will provide the surplus revenue which will be required to comply with the law, it will be extinguished wheher it is called a sinking fund or not. For the next year I have estimated the amount to be appropriated for the sinking fund, and it is to be hoped that the appropriations for general purposes will be kept down to such an extent that there will be sufficient surplus revenue to meet it.

I think we will have enough to cover the sinking fund for this year at the end of the fiscal year.

The CHAIRMAN. Do you not anticipate during the next six months an enormous importation?

Secretary SHERMAN. It is coming now; but then our exportations are increasing also.

The CHAIRMAN. I am only speaking of that fact in its connection with the question of revenue. Do you not think the exaltation of prices in this country and the depression that has been going on in Europe and is still continuing will necessarily send large quantities of European goods to this country?

Secretary SHERMAN. It looks like it now.

Mr. KERNAN. I see that during the eleven months up to last November our exportations have increased over the corresponding months for the preceding year $50,000,000.

Secretary SHERMAN. I think our surplus revenue for the first six months was taken up in payment of back pensions; but the revenue for the succeeding six months will be sufficient to meet the sinking fund, amounting to about $40,000,000.

Mr. BECK. I was thinking that the Secretary might desire to make his statements generally to-day and get them printed. I propose to inquire pretty carefully before we get through with this interview concerning the immense reduction of the public debt which has been made, of over $700,000,000, from the highest point down to the present, so that we may be governed in the future taxation by actual requirements of the public service. And I desire further to ascertain whether or not we have so far complied with the sinking-fund provision by the reduction of the debt, as shown in the reports of the different Secretaries, as to make it possible to dispense altogether with that fund, or, as the Secretary expresses it, the use of surplus revenue, in this manner. I believe that after the Secretary has made his general statements upon all these subjects, we could examine them carefully and continue the interview at some future day.

BONDS FOR REFUNDING.

Secretary SHERMAN. In reply to the general propositions submitted to me by the chairman as to the advantages of the different forms of loans, I beg to submit the following as my views:

1. The four per cent. is already a very popular bond both in Europe and in this country, and is largely used in paying balances between bankers and between countries, as well as for trust-fund and savings-institution investment.

2. Experience indicates that the rate of interest is as low as it can be if the bonds are to be kept at par. A statement of the issues of all the loans since the organization of the government is published in the financial report of 1876. From that statement it will be seen that the government has never been able to place a bond at as low a rate as four per cent. (until the recent operation), and in only a few instances as low as $4\frac{1}{2}$ per cent., and then for comparatively small amounts. I present here a table showing at what rate to investors the principal loans of the United States have been placed, excluding the loans of the late rebellion not sold for coin:

TABLE *showing the rates at which United States loans were placed on the market, together with the calculated rates of interest realized to investors, at different periods from 1796 to 1861, inclusive.*

Year placed on market.	Title of loan.	Rate of interest. (Per cent.)	Amount issued.	Price of sale. (Per cent.)	Years to run.	Rate realized. (Per cent.)
1796	Six per cent. stock of 1796	6	840,000 00	87¾	21	7.09
1798	Eight per cent. stock of 1798	8	5,000,000 00	Par.	15	8
1800	Eight per cent. stock of 1800	8	1,481,700 00	105.64	15	7.37
1807	Exchanged six per cent. stock of 1807	6	6,294,051 12	Par.	Indefinite.	6
1812	Six per cent. stock of 1812	6	8,134,700 00	Par.	13	6
1812	Exchanged six per cent. stock of 1812	6	2,984,746 72	Par.	12	6
1813	Sixteen million loan of 1813	6	*16,100,377 43	88	13	7.54
1813	Seven and one-half million loan of 1813	6	4,427,575 07	86.25	12	7.50
1814	Seven and one-half million loan of 1813	6	4,071,008 50	86.25	12	7.50
1814	Ten million loan of 1814	6	9,919,476 25	80	12	8.72
1814	Six million loan of 1814	6	5,384,134 87	80	12	6.51
1814	Undesignated loan of 1814	6	157,894 68	95	12	8.04
1814	Undesignated loan of 1814	6	147,058 81	85	11	7.20
1815	Undesignated loan of 1814	6	47,627 79	90.75	11	7.30
1815	Undesignated loan of 1814	6	62,420 72	90.50	11	8.64
1815	Undesignated loan of 1814	6	15,600 00	85	11	7.24
1816	Undesignated loan of 1814	6	87,912 06	91	10	9.09
1816	Undesignated loan of 1814	6	204,289 23	80	10	4.22
1821	Five per cent. stock of 1821	5	4,735,296 30	5.1 @ 8 prm.	13½	4¼
1824	Four and one-half per cent. stock of 1824, act of May 24, 1824	4½	5,000,000 00	Par.	8	4¼
1824	Four and one-half per cent. stock of 1824	4½	4,454,727 95	Par.	6 and 9	4¼
1824	Exchanged four and one-half per cent. stock of 1824, act May 26, 1824	4½	5,000,000 00	Par.	Indefinite.	4¼
1825	Exchanged four and one-half per cent. stock of 1825	4½	1,539,336 16	Par.	3 and 4	4¼
1842	Loan of 1842	6	8,343,886 03	97.50 to par.	20	6 to 6.22
1843	Loan of 1843	5	7,004,231 35	1 to 3.75 prm.	10	4.52 to 4.87
1846	Loan of 1846	6	4,999,149 45	Par.	10	
1847	Loan of 1847	6	28,207,000 00	1.25 @ 2 prm.	20	5.82 to 5.89
1848	Loan of 1848	6	16,000,000 00	3.02 @ 4 prm.	20	5.66 to 5.74
1858	Loan of 1858	5	20,000,000 00	Par.	15	5
1861	Loan of February, 1861	6	18,415,000 00	Par.	10 or 20	6
1861	Loan of July and August, 1861	6	189,321,300 00	Par.	20	6

*The amount of cash received on the loan was $16,000,000, of which amount $531,200 was placed at par with an annuity of 1¼ per cent, making the interest realized on the sixteen millions 7.50 per cent.

There is always a distinction to be made between the rate at which a loan can be sold in the market and the market rate of the bonds after the loan is placed.

The distribution of a loan among small and permanent investors even under the most favorable circumstances is never done without more or less help from capital, and that capital must be paid for making this distribution. Besides as long as loans are being sold in the market the supply can always equal the demand. Subsequent and unforseen events may make that loan desirable for some specific purpose and raise the price of it considerably above that for which it was sold, and that without any fault or lack of foresight on the part of the government selling the loan. In 1871 and 1872 France sold 5 per cent. bonds for 82 per cent. of their face value. The same bonds are now worth 114. I think it is safe to say that the government has at all times obtained the best price possible for the loans placed upon the market.

So long as the 4 per cent. bond was being sold it was with difficulty kept at par or within 1 per cent. of it. It fell at one time to 98 per cent., less than a year ago, and the associated bankers of London asked for an extension of time in which they were to make another subscription, giving as a reason that the bond was below par, and that they could not take it under the terms of their contract without loss. As soon, however, as all the 4 per cents were taken, and it was well understood that no more could be issued for refunding, for several years, the price began to advance and has reached at the present time about 4 per cent. above par. It could hardly be expected, however, that should additional amounts be placed upon the market that any such premium as this would be maintained.

Should the exchange of 4 per cents. for the 5s and 6s of 1881 be authorized as desired, the government would undoubtedly be able to exchange a large portion, if not the entire amount, of the outstanding fives and sixes without using depositary banks or syndicates to aid in the transaction, and without the payment of any double interest, the market value of the 4 per cents being so high that holders of sixes would be glad to exchange bond for bond; and the government cannot reasonably expect to make much better terms than these.

It is noticeable that there is not to-day a 3 per cent. or 3½ per cent. bond of any government which sells for par. Within the last century, the English 3 per cent. consols have sold as low as $47.20 for $100, yielding to the investor nearly 6½ per cent interest.

The rate of 4 per cent. per annum is probably the most convenient rate in the calculation of interest that can be established. On $100 the interest is even $4 a year. On each quarter year it is $1; and in days it is about 10 cents for 9 days. For a $50 bond it is, of course, one-half, the rates for $100. For numbers larger than $100 it will be a multiple of that rate, thus keeping the payments in even dollars, as far as practicable.

A 3.65 bond gives an odd number of cents for the year, and whether multiplied or divided, it still continues to give odd and fractional cents for the periods for which calculations must be made.

Of course this would have no special bearing where it is only a question whether you pay 3.65 or 4 per cent. interest, but it must be borne in mind that if a 4 per cent. bond is issued, the premium which can be obtained therefrom will determine the rate of interest realized by investors; and the amount which the government would in the end be compelled to pay for the loan will be substantially the same whether it is a 3.65 or a 4 per cent. bond.

Again, we have $740,000,000 of 4 per cent. bonds out. Owing to the large amount outstanding the loan is necessarily distributed over a wide extent of country, and among a great many people, being a continual advertisement of itself, and really giving it a larger value than it would have if it were but little known; and if a 3.65 bond, or a bond bearing any other rate of interest is thrown on the market, the government will probably not be able to sell it as advantageously as it could the 4s which are now so widely known.

In my opinion there would not be, in placing a 3.65 loan, any opposition from bankers, for it is a well-known fact that the greater variety of loans there are in the market the more money bankers can make through brokerage by exchanges of investments, as one class of bonds or another appear to offer better inducements as an investment. Thus the only persons likely to profit from placing any new description of loans in the market will be the bankers, brokers, and parties through whom the exchanges of bonds in the market are made.

It is important that the issue of the 4 per cents, or whatever bonds are to be authorized, should be commenced at once. On a sale of 4s we now realize a sufficient premium to pay the extra interest on the 5 and 6 per cent. bonds, thus enabling the government to exchange them bond for bond. In this way we shall take advantage of a present and certain condition of things to reduce, perhaps, $750,000,000 of the indebtedness from 6 and 5 per cent. to 4 per cent. per annum.

Authority to issue the 4s would make refunding a certainty from the start, which, I believe, would not be the case if any other bond should be authorized; and with authority to issue 4s the possibility of being forced to pay a higher rate after 1881 can be avoided.

While we cannot foresee the future, it is not believed by any one that a lower rate of interest is likely to prevail next year or the year after than now exists. On the other hand there is great danger that the rate of interest in this country may advance. New railroads, buildings, and business enterprises of all kinds are being pushed, and they all require capital; and with the present resources of the country this capital can be made to pay better than 4 per cent. interest; and when confidence is fully restored there is no reason to believe that people will be willing to accept 4 per cent. in lieu of 6 or 8 per cent. on their investments. Bad crops during the present year would materially change the aspect of our foreign trade, and with the resulting unfavorable exchanges, we may find ourselves in the midst of a restricted money market which would preclude borrowing at even 4 per cent.

It is well known that a large amount of the 5s and the 6s which might now be exchanged for 4s are in the hands of banks and bankers who are not at all anxious to surrender them. Apprehensions that steps might be taken towards the exchange of these bonds caused them in the early winter to fall until owners would, on the basis of their payment when due, obtain only about 4 per cent. interest; but in view of the delay in the action of Congress in this matter, and a growing belief that the bonds would not eventually be paid till sometime after they were due, they have again advanced, and the indications are that they are now principally held by bankers and large institutions, who have thus profited by the recent rise in this class of securities, and who hope to hold on to them still longer.

Again, we are to consider that the issue of national-bank notes is based upon the government bond as collateral. On every $100 par value of bonds the bank is entitled to receive not to exceed 90 per cent. in notes. Should the banks be permitted to deposit 3.65 bonds as

4 SH

collateral for circulation the notes received would not be as well secured as they are at present. It is possible that bonds might so decline in value that the holders of notes might not be secure.

OBJECTIONS TO THE 3½ OR 3.65 BONDS.

In the first place there is no certainty of our being able to sell either one of these bonds at par. Before a 3.65-bond can be sold at par, the 4 would necessarily have to be sold at 109, in order to realize the same rate of interest to the investor. They are now selling at 104, at which price they yield 3.76 per cent., probably the lowest rate of interest ever known in this country. I submit some tables bearing on this matter which speak for themselves.

TABLE showing, in New York, for December 4, 1879, the market prices, (or including the accrued interest) of the several classes of securities of the United States Government; the net prices of the same (or prices not including the interest accrued); the actual and estimated periods to payment; the corresponding rates of interest realized to investors; and the corresponding net prices of 3½ per cent. bonds having thirty years and fifty years, respectively, to run to payment.

Designation of securities.	Interest payable. First day of—	Principal payable.	Prices of securities December 4, 1879.		Period to payment, actual and estimated.	Computed rate of interest realized to investors (pr. ct.).	Corresponding net price of 3½ per cent. bonds having to run—	
			Including accrued interest (flat).	Not including accrued interest, (net).			30 years.	50 years.
6s of 1880	January and July	December 31, 1880	104.75	102.17	1 year	3.79	94.85	93.55
6s of 1881	January and July	At option of government: After June 30, 1881	106.375	103.79	1½ years	3.39	102.10	102.71
5s of 1881	F., M., A., and N.	After April 30, 1881	102.75	102.26	1½	3.70	96.42	95.50
					2	4.01	91.15	89.04
4½s of 1891	M., J., S., and D.	After August 31, 1891	105.50	105.44	1½	3.44	101.14	101.44
					2	3.82	93.99	92.93
4s of 1907	J., A., J., and O.	After June 30, 1907	103.125	102.40	2¼	4.04	90.68	88.47
					12	3.93	92.49	90.67
					28	3.86	93.67	92.11
Currency 6s:								
Payable, 1895	January and July		120.—	119.92	16 years	4.27	87.05	84.16
Payable, 1896	January and July		120.25	120.17	17	4.31	86.46	83.47
Payable, 1897	January and July		120.50	120.42	18	4.35	85.46	82.74
Payable, 1898	January and July		121.—	120.92	19	4.37	85.56	82.43
Payable, 1899	January and July		121.50	121.42	20	4.38	85.42	82.96

The rates for the bonds payable in 1881 have materially advanced since the above date.

TABLE *showing by months, quarter-years, half-years, and years during the calendar years 1878, and 1879, relative to the FOUR PER CENT. securities of the United States, their average prices in open market, both including the accrued interest (flat); and not including the same (net); the computed rate of interest realized to investors, and the corresponding net prices of 3½ per cent. bonds having thirty years and fifty years, respectively, to run to payment.*

[Interest payable January 1, April 1, July 1, and October 1. The United States four per cent. securities are redeemable at the option of the government at any time after June 30, 1907.]

Months, quarter-years, half-years, and calendar-years.	Average prices of securities.		Period assumed to run to payment.	Corresponding annual rate of interest realized to investors.	Corresponding net prices of 3½ per cent. securities having to run—	
	Including accrued interest (flat).	Not including accrued interest (net).			Thirty years to payment.	Fifty years to payment.
1878.			*Years.*	*Per cent.*		
January	101.69	101.52	29½	3.91	92.83	91.08
February	101.94	101.45	29½	3.92	92.66	90.87
March	101.54	100.71	29½	3.96	91.98	90.05
April	100.43	100.27	29	3.98	91.65	89.64
May	100.81	100.32	29	3.99	91.65	89.64
June	10k.21	100.38	29	3.99	91.48	89.44
July	100.42	100.25	29	3.99	91.48	89.44
August	100.675	100.17	29	3.99	91.48	89.44
September	100.94	100.11	29	3.99	91.48	89.44
October	99.875	99.70	28½	4.02	90.99	88.75
November	100.28	99.78	28½	4.01	91.05	89.04
December	100.51	99.68	28½	4.02	90.99	88.75
1879.						
January	99.86	99.69	28½	4.02	90.99	88.85
February	100.22	99.73	28½	4.017	91.04	88.91
March	99.47	98.64	28½	4.08	90.04	87.72
April	99.70	99.54	28	4.03	90.83	88.66
May	102.76	102.27	28	3.87	93.50	91.90
June	102.70	101.87	28	3.89	93.16	91.49
July	102.06	101.89	28	3.89	93.16	91.49
August	101.51	101.01	28	3.94	92.32	90.46
September	101.95	101.12	28	3.94	92.32	90.46
October	102.20	102.03	27½	3.88	93.33	91.70
November	103.00	102.50	27½	3.85	93.84	92.31
December	103.67	102.84	27½	3.83	94.05	92.06
1878.						
First quarter-year average		101.23	29½	3.93	92.49	90.67
Second quarter-year average		100.32	29	3.99	91.59	89.57
Third quarter-year average		100.18	29	3.99	91.48	89.44
Fourth quarter-year average		99.72	28½	4.02	91.00	88.88
1879.						
First quarter-year average		99.35	28½	4.04	90.69	88.49
Second quarter-year average		101.23	28	3.93	92.49	90.68
Third quarter-year average		101.34	28	3.92	92.60	90.80
Fourth quarter-year average		102.46	27½	3.85	93.74	92.02
1878.						
First half-year average		100.77	29¼	3.96	92.04	90.12
Second half-year average		99.95	28¾	4.00	91.24	89.14
1879.						
First half-year average		100.29	28¼	3.98	91.60	89.59
Second half-year average		101.90	27¾	3.89	93.17	91.41
Calendar year:						
1878		100.36	28	3.98	91.64	89.63
1879		100.05	29	3.93	92.39	90.50

It is admitted by all persons who desire to place the 3½s or 3.65s, that such bonds must have a term of 50 years to run, in order to make a success of the loan. It has always been the policy of our government to make its loans as short as practicable, or at least to give the government control of them after a comparatively brief period. It may be that within 30 years our surplus revenues will be sufficient to enable us to pay off the proposed loan, and in such a case the hands of the government should not be tied. The wisdom of the policy which has heretofore been pursued, of giving the government an option in the redemption of these loans after a few years, has been already well demonstrated. Only by the reservation of this option has the refunding of the past few years and the consequent reduction of interest of nearly $20,000,000 per annum under its operation been possible.

If, at the end of 30 years, the government should wish to take up the $750,000,000 of 4 per cents proposed to be issued hereafter for refunding purposes, it will then have paid $950,000,000 of interest; but if a 3½ per cent. bond should be issued for 50 years, without option, government would be compelled to pay over $1,300,000,000; if a 3.65 bond, nearly $1,400,000,000 in interest before the bonds could be paid off at par; or about $500,000,000 more than if a 4 per cent. bond should be issued for 30 years. Should our sinking-fund be kept up as now required by law, the debt will be wiped out in about 30 years, and the $500,000,000 would thus be saved to the people.

Mr. ALLISON. That expresses your view as to what we ought to do in the future.

Mr. BECK. Have you stated anything anywhere about the mode of placing the loan? I thought we made a great success in that loan (the refunding certificates), which approached nearer to a popular loan than any other. How far could you reach the masses in that way?

Secretary SHERMAN. You can do it easily. It would be necessary to modify the bill introduced by Mr. Morrill in one particular. That bill continues the law which authorizes the sale of refunding certificates at par for cash. We ought rather to sell these certificates, which are convertible into 4 per cent. bonds, for the same premium that the bonds themselves sell for; a premium that will enable the department to obtain the 5s. and 6s. which it desires to refund. It would be a great transaction, and one of much value to the government. But under the provisions of this pending bill I could not dispose of these refunding certificates to the people to whom I would sell them, as they are not the ones who would in return give me bonds. The people, whom we want to get these certificates, not having the bonds, if we should sell them the certificates for money, what could we do with the money?

Mr. FERRY. Could you not turn right around and sell the four per cents for four per cent. premium.

Secretary SHERMAN. I could only do it in exchange.

Mr. FERRY. Suppose you receive cash and then you retire the bonds —it is a different process, but you reach the same end.

Secretary SHERMAN. We can do that. But suppose I sell a million of refunding certificates, not getting a million of bonds, I would increase the public debt.

Mr. MORRILL. You must authorize him to sell the four per cent. certificates at a premium.

Mr. BECK suggested that the Secretary's views on this point be put in shape and presented to the committee.

Mr. MORRILL. A better method would be for the department to prepare a suitable bill.

Mr. BECK. But that would not explain itself to us.

Secretary SHERMAN. The bill you have here covers the whole ground, except so far as refunding certificates are concerned.

Mr. BECK. I think it would be better for the Secretary to add an explanation about the refunding certificates.

Mr. ALLISON. I think it is desirable to have this certificate feature added, and if you can work it properly we perhaps might incorporate it into the law.

Secretary SHERMAN. We can do that.

Mr. BECK. Whether we think it advisable or not, I think it is extremely desirable that this committee should have the Secretary's opinions about the matter, in case it should come before the Senate, and there may be persons, and I may be one of them, who will entertain that view, and who will like to know what there is for and against it.

Mr. FERRY. Could you not purchase the five per cent. bonds and then make one clear the other?

Secretary SHERMAN. Suppose I cannot purchase enough, then I would have to increase the public debt. All these loans are coupled with the conditions that I must not increase that debt. It is a pretty large authority to allow the sale of bonds without limit as to price; as long as you allow the sale of bonds so as to buy the bonds desired to be redeemed at no expense to the government there is no danger.

Mr. BECK. I observe in all your funding operations you have to temporarily increase the public debt when the two classes of bonds are outstanding.

Secretary SHERMAN. Temporarily increase the bonded debt, but we do not increase the aggregate debt because we deduct the money on hand.

Mr. KERNAN. That is, the receipts from sales of bonds are put as a credit against bonds not redeemed.

Mr. BECK. For example, on the 28th of February, 1879, I look at the monthly statement of last year and the principal of the interest-bearing debt of the United States was $2,014,000,000, while the debt less cash in the Treasury was $2,026,000,000, thus showing that every dollar of the debt of the United States was paying interest on that day except about $12,000,000.

Secretary SHERMAN. That was caused by the sale of $216,628,200 of 4 per cent. bonds, for which bonds had been called but had not matured, as fully set forth on that statement.

The CHAIRMAN. What is the length of time when the bonds sold and the bond called in refunding operations both draw interest?

Secretary SHERMAN. From the date of sale of bonds sold to the time of maturity of the bonds called.

The CHAIRMAN. That is the extreme limit of time during which both bonds could draw interest?

Secretary SHERMAN. As I explained to you, I avoided that somewhat by calling in advance, and by that means I reduced this limit of double-interest time to about 60 days. It cannot be any more than 90 days. In 1877, as I said before, I came very near being caught with fifteen millions called in advance.

You will find that other governments pay from two to three per cent. commission, and that no other government has sold bonds with such pecuniary advantage as we have.

The CHAIRMAN. Do they not require notice?

Secretary SHERMAN. England has sold her three per cent. bonds seldom at par, and some have been sold so low down that they yielded an interest of six and a half per cent. to the investor. They do not care anything about the principal of the public debt; they only look to see what interest they must pay.

Mr. MORRILL. But they are being scored on all sides lately in relation to their public debt. When Gladstone and Bright contrast their financial policy with the American policy of paying debts, the English policy does not loom up very well.

The committee then adjourned.

APPENDIX A.

WASHINGTON, *April* 26, 1879.

The CHAIRMAN. Before proceeding to the main subject of this conference I wish to ask some questions in relation to the trade-dollar. Can you give us, Mr. Secretary, a correct statement or estimate of the number of trade-dollars now in the United States?

Secretary SHERMAN. I can state that the amount of trade-dollars that have been coined is $35,959,300. The amount of them exported, as shown by the statistics we have, partly estimated but nearly accurate, may be said to be about twenty-nine million dollars. These are about the figures that were given in my annual report in December last, and I believe they are as nearly accurate as possible. This would leave in the country between six and seven millions of trade-dollars.

Mr. CLAFLIN. Is there any evidence that any of those have been taken up, used as bullion or any other way?

Secretary SHERMAN. We have no evidence on that point. It is hardly probable, however, that they would be, because bullion has been cheaper all the time than trade-dollars.

The CHAIRMAN. Is there any serious objection to taking up those trade-dollars and giving standard silver dollars for them and then recoining them—never issuing them again?

Secretary SHERMAN. I think the objections are very serious. There are three radical objections, any one of which, I think, ought to prevent the government from taking that course. First, it would be a discrimination against our own miners in the price of silver bullion and in favor of the holders of these dollars in China. At least from twenty-six to twenty-eight millions of these trade-dollars are held in China as bullion. The trade-dollars were coined as bullion and sold as bullion, for private parties, for private profit, and the government had no connection with them except to charge the actual cost to the owners of the bullion. They had a limited legal-tender quality until July 22, 1876, but they did not get into circulation in this country until October, 1876; so that every trade-dollar that is now in circulation in this country was put in circulation at a time when it was not a legal tender, but simply represented 420 grains of standard silver. If we should now make it exchangeable for the standard silver dollar, and equal to the gold dollar, it would be worth for that purpose 14 or 15 cents more than it is worth as bullion, and the owners of this bullion in China, or the purchasers of those coins for the purpose of bringing them here, would get the benefit of that difference. We can buy the same amount of silver bullion from our own miners to-day for four or five millions of dollars less than we can get this bullion in China, if the proposed measure should become a law. That is the first objection.

Mr. WARNER. Would that objection, however, lie if silver was admitted to free or unlimited coinage in the United States?

Secretary SHERMAN. No; if silver coinage is made free at the rate of 16 of silver to 1 of gold, we shall have a mono-metallic system of silver coinage, excluding gold from circulation. Then, as a matter of course, the objection would cease; then the trade-dollar would be worth more than the standard dollar. That is, if you adopt the bullion value of silver as the sole standard in this country, then it makes no difference what is done with the trade-dollar; but as long as you maintain the gold standard or the present standard, based upon the gold coin of 25 8/10 grains, the introduction of the trade-dollar, either as a coin or as the equal of the standard dollar, will be a discrimination in favor of the owners of this silver bullion in China and against our own miners to the extent that I have stated.

Mr. WARNER. That is, while silver is coined under existing law and regulations?

Secretary SHERMAN. Certainly. The chairman did not ask me about my views in regard to the question of bi-metallic or mono-metallic money.

The CHAIRMAN. Suppose we change our system in relation to the coinage of silver and make it unrestricted, so that the government will not purchase bullion at all; suppose that the system of purchasing bullion for coin is abrogated and the unlimited coinage of silver is introduced, then ought not the trade-dollar and the legal-tender standard dollar to be interchangeable?

Secretary SHERMAN. If Congress should finally determine to adopt the silver standard——

The CHAIRMAN. The double standard?

Secretary SHERMAN. Yes; the free coinage of both gold and silver upon the present ratios. If that is to be adopted, then the proposition is not objectionable; but that brings up at once the great question whether that ought to be done.

The CHAIRMAN. That is the point we have before us, and I understand that in case we do that, your opinion is that then the trade-dollar and the standard silver dollar ought to be interchangeable.

Secretary SHERMAN. Yes; but in case you should do that, no man of ordinary sagacity would surrender a trade-dollar for the standard dollar; he would want to receive the difference between them. You would not be able to get the trade-dollar exchanged for the standard dollar, because the trade-dollar contains 420 grains of silver, while the standard dollar contains only 412½.

The CHAIRMAN. Then you would not be bothered with the recoining?

Secretary SHERMAN. No. The trade-dollar would be, as the old Mexican dollar was formerly, a little more valuable than our standard dollar.

Mr. WARNER. It would simply go to the mint as bullion?

Secretary SHERMAN. Hardly; it would not be exchanged on an equality with the standard dollar.

The CHAIRMAN. What amount of standard silver dollars coined since the act of last year are now in circulation?

Secretary SHERMAN. According to latest returns received at the department there have been coined of these dollars $30,542,950. We have now on hand $22,887,695; leaving $7,655,255 of those dollars in circulation.

The CHAIRMAN. How many coin-certificates have been issued under the act of 1878?

Secretary SHERMAN. An amount of $10,437,000. Nearly all our silver bullion is purchased by silver-certificates, but then they are at once returned to the Treasury.

The CHAIRMAN. I understand you to say that there are very few of them out now?

Secretary SHERMAN. Very few. They are at once converted. They come right back.

Mr. WARNER. They come back in payment of duties?

Secretary SHERMAN. Largely in payment of bonds, and also for the payment of duties. The whole amount outstanding now is only $176,330.

The CHAIRMAN. In connection with the sales of bonds that have been made lately?

Secretary SHERMAN. Yes; lately and all along.

The CHAIRMAN. What would be the objection to issuing coin-certificates down to denominations of fives, and threes, and twos, and ones, and halves, and quarters, for change?

Secretary SHERMAN. The objection to issuing coin-certificates while you have legal tender notes outstanding is that the coin-certificates, of whatever denomination they may be, will not circulate while the legal-tender notes are outstanding. Until the 1st of January the coin-certificates had the advantage over the legal-tender notes, because they were receivable for bonds, for customs duties, and for all purposes, and therefore they had a special value or use which the legal-tender notes had not; but now the legal-tender notes are, in effect, a coin-certificate, and may be used for all purposes. There is now no occasion for coin-certificates, which come back into the Treasury.

Mr. VANCE. Then can they not be put out again?

Secretary SHERMAN. They can, but we have "greenbacks," which we are bound to keep in circulation, and which fill all the channels of circulation under existing law. It would be difficult to keep the two forms of currency afloat at the same time. If either were taken away, then the other would fill the channels of circulation.

Mr. WARNER. Is there any objection to those certificates if persons holding bullion or coin prefer the certificates to handling the coin or bullion, even though the certificates may come back, as coin would, in payment of duties to the government?

The CHAIRMAN. The question I meant to ask is this: Is there any practical objection to issuing coin-certificates, if persons prefer them, so as to get rid of these fractional silver dollars; in other words, is there any objection to having coin-certificates ready to exchange with any persons who prefer them, down to the denominations of fives, ones, halves, and quarters?

Secretary SHERMAN. If you issue them in small sums there is the same objection that was made always to the fractional currency, that it was very perishable and very costly, and a great loss to the people on account of its being so perishable.

The CHAIRMAN. Would they be more perishable, or a greater loss to the government, or more costly after the plates are made, than the coin itself is? Is not the waste and abrasion of the coin itself quite as great as that of the fractional currency?

Secretary SHERMAN. Experience shows that it is not. The fractional currency was found to last only about fifteen or eighteen months, while silver coin lasts in circulation about twenty-three years, and gold coin about fifty years. The actual cost of the fractional currency in the last year or two before it was abandoned was shown to be about three per cent. per annum, and that currency perished in about fifteen or eighteen months on an average.

The CHAIRMAN. But you would have the plates, so that there would be no cost in replacing it except for the paper?

Secretary SHERMAN. Yes; but on ten-cent and twenty-five cent currency the cost, even of a million, is considerable.

The CHAIRMAN. I would not have the denominations go below twenty-five cents. You speak of gold coin wearing fifty years, and silver coin a much less time; how do you account for that?

Secretary SHERMAN. That, I suppose, is because the gold coin passes through fewer hands.

The CHAIRMAN. We had a statement here the other day about a double-eagle which was weighed in the Treasury Department and found to have lost seven grains.

Secretary SHERMAN. It must have undergone pretty rapid and extensive usage.

The CHAIRMAN. Mr. Riggs, I understand, says that his loss is immense on gold coin, because the Treasury will not take it from him except by weight, and his loss thereby is several per cent.

Secretary SHERMAN. There are statistical tables in the reports of the Director of the Mint which show very accurately the amount of abrasion of different coins. Gold coin, from the fact that it does not circulate so freely, lasts longer than any other.

The CHAIRMAN. I understand your answer to my question to amount to this: that there is no practical objection to issuing these coin certificates except the increased cost.

Secretary SHERMAN. As to the fractional notes, the objection is one of cost and wear and tear. Another objection is this: I think the instinctive desire of men generally, especially laboring men, is to handle the coin itself. I think this desire is better gratified by the sense of touch in handling coin than in handling paper.

The CHAIRMAN. My question does not go to that extent, because it leaves it optional with people to have the one or the other as they prefer. Is there any practical objection to the government being ready to issue these certificates if the holders of coin or bullion shall so desire?

Secretary SHERMAN. I do not think that the double system is wise. If you adopt the one you should reject the other. The double system puts us to the great expense of maintaining mints to supply the coin, and also the Bureau of Engraving and Printing to supply the paper. In my judgment it is better to have either the one or the other, not both. Many very intelligent people, bankers as well as others, do, I know, prefer small fractional currency to silver currency.

There is another grave objection to the issue of coin certificates, that they will inevitably replace and destroy the legal-tender notes, or compel the suspension of specie payments on such notes. In case of the slightest suspicion or doubt of the ability to maintain redemption, or in case brokers or bankers choose for speculative purposes to make gold scarce, they may, without cost or trouble, or without handling the coin, present legal-tender notes to the Treasury and demand coin, and turn over the coin for certificates. Upon issuing the certificates the Treasury must keep the full amount of coin for the payment of the certificates, thus reducing the coin reserve for the payment of United States notes, and throwing upon the Treasury the risk and expense of keeping the coin for private and perhaps hostile purposes. It was this very danger that induced me to decline in December last to issue any more gold certificates. One protection to the Treasury is the inconvenience to which the parties presenting the coins would be put in receiving and hoarding them, but if the issue of certificates is made mandatory, a few active brokers might convert all the coin in the Treasury into certificates, and leave no means with which to redeem United States notes. I can see no public interest that would be promoted by a mandatory issue of coin certificates in exchange for gold or silver bullion, and if they are issued without an actual deposit of coin, to be held for their redemption, they are only another form of United States notes.

The CHAIRMAN. One other question. What do you think of having ingots of gold or silver, say silver, of the value of $100, assayed, refined, and stamped, for purposes of exchange, instead of coin? Do you or no think that such ingots would answer the purpose of a medium of exchange with other countries, to be used instead of coin in settling balances—I mean ingots of pure silver or gold? Dr. Linderman made the suggestion to us last year, and that is why I want to get your views on the subject now. If that were done, there would be no drain from abroad upon our coinage. These ingots would be resorted to instead.

Secretary SHERMAN. We have ingots of gold and silver now. In the assay office in New York you will see great ingots of gold and silver of various denominations and values, with the values stamped upon them, just as you suggest.

The CHAIRMAN. But they are not of the same denominations as the coin?

Secretary SHERMAN. No.

The CHAIRMAN. The suggestion was to have them of the same denominations, and to have them all alike, fine ingots of silver of $100 each, with $100 worth of silver in them, measured by our standard dollar. Dr. Linderman's idea was that those ingots would be used in commerce, for the purposes I have suggested, without a resort to coin.

Secretary SHERMAN. That is rather a question of convenience. It is to provide coin of the denomination of $100 or ten eagles.

The CHAIRMAN. The idea was, I believe, that when those ingots went abroad the foreign mints would not be troubled with our alloy, because the ingot would be pure silver.

Secretary SHERMAN. Well, that is a technical question which I do not pretend to know much about—whether it is better to export silver in the pure state or not. Most of the bullion in the mint and at the assay office is gold or silver with a shade of alloy; then when coined they add the proper alloy to conform to the law of the country.

The CHAIRMAN. I will put the same question to Mr. Burchard, the Director of the Mint, whether he has given any attention to that point.

Mr. BURCHARD. I have not, particularly. The question of stamping a value upon silver bars has not been raised or considered since I have had charge of the Mint Bureau.

The CHAIRMAN. I wish, Mr. Secretary, that you and Mr. Burchard, when the notes of this conference are submitted to you, will add anything that may occur to you in the mean time upon this point.

Mr. BURCHARD. A person bringing silver bullion now to the mint and desiring to have it converted into fine bars is entitled to have that done, and to have fine silver bars delivered to him in lieu of the bullion. The value is not stamped upon such silver bars, but simply the weight and fineness. That is now the course of business at the coinage mints and at New York assay office.

Mr. WARNER. And the only limit under the law now is that nothing shall be stamped less than five ounces; which would be a very small bar of silver.

Mr. VANCE. What is the trade-dollar worth at the Treasury now, Mr. Secretary? At what rate do you receive it in place of bullion.

Secretary SHERMAN. We are not authorized to receive it at all except as bullion; the bullion value is now 85.8. The commercial value among the brokers is 98.75. We would buy it as bullion, if it was offered, at one cent under the market rate, because we buy at one cent less than the bullion value when offered in small lots, but in large lots we buy at the market rate for bullion.

Mr. VANCE. What is the probable amount of the fractional coin now in circulation?

Secetary SHERMAN. The exact amount of fractional silver in circulation cannot be given. Of the amount which has been paid out since January 1, 1875, there is now outstanding $11,485,433.56, and the amount now on hand at the several mints and assistant treasurers' offices is $6,598,492.44.

Mr. FISHER. To pursue the inquiry of the chairman a step further: What would you think of the idea of the issuance of silver-certificates of the denomination of one dollar and two dollars? There is a scarcity of legal-tender notes of those denominations in the country.

Secretary SHERMAN. I think the objections to issuing silver-certificates or gold-certificates of any denominations while United States notes are in circulation are very clear. As to the scarcity of United States notes of small denominations, that is simply because persons who come to the Treasury for money will not take them. We issue ones and twos freely, but hardly anybody wants them. Any one who chooses can come to the Treasury with a draft for $100 or $1,000, and get every dollar of it in one-dollar notes if he wishes.

Mr. FISHER. Can that be done now?

Secretary SHERMAN. Certainly, and it could always be done. I know that a stringency does occur in some localities, because the great transactions with the government require large sums of money, and people prefer notes of large denominations because it is easier to carry large sums of money in that form. Always, since I have been in the department, I have taken great pains to distribute ones and twos, and any person receiving money can get any number of them he wishes to carry away at any time.

Mr. FISHER. In my section of Pennsylvania we have been suffering from a scarcity of those small notes. You have spoken of people preferring coin to paper; now, our people consider the silver dollar a nuisance.

Secretary SHERMAN. I think the silver dollar is rather too large for change. I was speaking rather of the subsidiary coinage. But so far as the one and two dollar notes are concerned, I am very glad to state, and to have it generally known, that anybody can get as many of them at the Treasury as he wants, either in payment of draft or in exchange for larger sums.

Mr. FISHER. I have heard it said that the Treasury took in the smaller notes and issued only the larger ones, and I am glad to know from the Secretary that we can get the smaller denominations.

Secretary SHERMAN. I have endeavored to promote the circulation of the ones and twos in every way that I could.

Mr. CLAFLIN. The difficulty in keeping the small legal-tender notes in circulation is that the banks, having to keep a reserve, gather up the legal tenders and do not pay them out, but put them in the Treasury. That is because they do not issue ones and twos of their own. If they issued ones and twos of their own, the legal tenders would be freely circulated; but as it is, the tendency must be for them to go into the bank reserves.

The CHAIRMAN. But why don't they pay them out?

Mr. CLAFLIN. Because they have to keep from 10 to 25 per cent. reserve, and they do not want to go and get gold and silver and pay out the ones and twos; they prefer to hold the small notes for their reserve. That is the difficulty.

Mr. FISHER. That is not the difficulty with us. The difficulty in our section is that the ones and twos have been worn out and have gone in for redemption, and we have not received others in return of the same small denominations to supply their places.

Mr. CLAFLIN. That is, your bank notes, ones and twos, that were in circulation have gone home, and the department has sent back five-dollar notes, or notes of some other larger denomination, in the place of the ones and twos.

Mr. FISHER. Then it is only a question of time when they will all go out of circulation.

Mr. CLAFLIN. It is only a question of time in regard to the ones and twos.

Secretary SHERMAN. There never was more than between five and six millions of small bank notes in circulation, while we have from forty to fifty millions of small United States notes in circulation.

Mr. CLAFLIN. But those are all held by the banks; they are not in circulation.

Secretary SHERMAN. We give ones and twos for fives, tens, and hundreds, and pay them out when called for.

Mr. CLAFLIN. But the natural result is that they are held by the banks for reserves.

Mr. WARNER. Has there been, then, within the last year, or since the act of May 31, 1878, any absolute contraction in the amount of one and two dollar legal-tender notes in circulation? Is the amount absolutely any less now than a year ago?

Secretary SHERMAN. In answer to that I will give you a table, showing the exact amount of ones and twos out May 31, 1878, and at the present date.

Date.	Denomination.	Amount.	Date.	Denomination.	Amount.
May 31, 1878	Ones	$31,576,728 80	Apr. 26, 1879	Ones	$18,953,172 80
May 31, 1878	Twos	21,601,458 20	Apr. 26, 1879	Twos	18,871,394 20

Mr. WILLIS. Mr. Secretary, in answer to the first question which was put to you by the chairman you said that there were three objections to the recoinage of the trade-dollar. You stated one, and were i nterrupted before you had completed the statement of those objectio ns. I should be very glad to have you now state the other two.

Secretary SHERMAN. The second objection is that it would b_r ing us abruptly to the single silver standard. The few millions of trade, dollars now in circulation are very unpopular and cause the demand to C ongress to get rid of them. If you now make them lawful money, or authorize them to be converted at par into lawful money, the largest part of the 30 millions exported will be presented for redemption in the standard silver dollars. If you force the standard silver dollars into circulation, I know by experience they will at once come back for taxes and bonds, and as often as reissued will come back, until we will be driven to hoard them in our vaults, or they will drag our paper money down to the market value of silver bullion and will expel gold. This will create wide and sweeping changes in contracts. For forty years all contracts have been based upon gold coin, except since the issue of legal-tender notes. Now these are at par with gold coin, and thus far we have maintained our silver coin at the same standard because the amount was limited and the supply mainly in the Treasury. The addition of 30 millions of trade-dollars to our active circulation, together with the continued coinage of two millions a month of standard dollars, would soon force into use the silver dollar as the sole standard of value for all paper money and for all contracts. If this is to be done it should be directly, by free coinage, when all silver bullion would have an equal chance, and not by discriminating in favor of bullion in a trade-dollar, every one of which now in circulation in this country is a fraud upon the law. My view of this trade-dollar was given last year in a letter which was published, and was better expressed than I can in this conversation. If you will allow me, I will hand it to the reporter.

TREASURY DEPARTMENT,
OFFICE OF THE SECRETARY,
Washington, D. C., September 3, 1878.

SIR: I hasten to fulfill the promise I made you that upon my return to the department I would write you fully concerning the issue of the trade-dollar and the present depreciation in its value.

The coinage of this dollar was authorized by the coinage act of February 12, 1873, in words as follows:

"That any owner of silver bullion may deposit the same at any mint to be formed into bars or into dollars of the weight of four hundred and twenty grains troy, designated in this act as trade-dollars, * * * and the charges for converting standard silver into trade-dollars, for melting and refining, when bullion is below standard, for toughening when metals are contained in it which render it unfit for coinage, for copper used for alloy, when the bullion is above standard, for separating the gold and silver when these metals exist together in the bullion, and for the preparation of bars, shall be fixed from time to time by the Director [of the Mint], with the concurrence of the Secretary of the Treasury, so as to equal, but not exceed, in their judgment, the actual average cost to each mint and assay office of the material, labor, wastage, and use of machinery employed in each of the cases aforementioned."

As its name indicates, the purpose of this coin was for *trade*, not for circulation, though by classifying it with other silver coins the law made it a legal tender to the amount of five (5) dollars in any one payment.

At the time of the passage of the act the actual value of this dollar, including the charge of 1¼ cents for coinage, was a little more than $1.04 in gold.

Under such circumstances there could be no object for the owner to put the coins into circulation, and consequently they were exported mostly to China, where, from lack of a circulating medium, these pieces, convenient in size, and bearing the guarantee of a great government as to their weight and fineness, obtained an extensive circulation, and created a market for the silver of the Pacific States, as intended by the act.

After a few months, however, an unforeseen depreciation in the value of silver bullion occurred, and in the early part of 1876 this depreciation reached such a point that one dollar in gold would purchase more than the necessary amount of silver for a trade-dollar and pay for its coinage.

Under such conditions dealers in bullion found a profit in putting trade-dollars into circulation at par in the Pacific States, where the currency was upon a gold basis, but the coin being a legal tender for only five (5) dollars, its circulation was necessarily limited in amount as well as restricted in locality.

The people of the Pacific States, however, objected to its use at all for circulation, and the attention of Congress having been called to the matter, on the 8th of May, 1876, Hon. Samuel J. Randall, of Pennsylvania, introduced into the House a bill the third section of which repealed the legal-tender quality of these coins.

On the 10th of June following, Hon. S. S. Cox, of New York, reported the measure to the House, urging its adoption.

No objection was raised, and it became a law July 22, 1876, without modification or an opposing voice or vote in either House, and is as follows:

"That the trade-dollar shall not hereafter be a legal tender; and the Secretary of the Treasury is hereby authorized to limit, from time to time, the coinage thereof to such an amount as he may deem sufficient to meet the export demand for the same."

Up to that time (excepting a few days), and for several months thereafter, the trade-dollar cost more than a paper currency dollar, and consequently none of the coins got into circulation in other than the Pacific States.

Owing to the appreciation of the paper currency, however, in the fall of 1877, the trade-dollar became of less value than the paper dollar, and in December of that year a large number of them were put into circulation, at their face value, at a profit to the owners of the bullion.

Apprehensive of such misuse of the coins, on the 15th of October in that year I ordered the discontinuance of their coinage at the mint at Philadelphia, and four days later at the other mints. Meanwhile the department, in reply to numerous inquiries, had uniformly stated that the trade-dollar possessed only a commercial value depending upon the price of silver bullion.

It will be seen that the coins were put into circulation months after the passage of the act taking from them their legal-tender character, and mainly after their coinage had ceased.

But in their use as money the department has never had any interest or derived any profit. For the expense of their coinage the owner of the bullion reimbursed the government, and this ended the connection of the government with the transaction. At no time and on no account have they ever been received, or paid out, by the Treasury, and it is a cause of regret that so many of our people should have accepted them at their face value, thus enabling their owners to put them into circulation at a considerable profit.

Under date of July 25, 1878, the Director of the Mint published tables from which the value of these coins can be ascertained and the terms on which they are received at the mints. He does not advise any one to dispose of them at such rates. The law under which the department buys bullion with which to coin the standard silver dollar requires the same to be bought at the market price, and it can purchase trade-dollars only as bullion. Possibly in time these coins will find a ready market in China, at nearly or quite their face value, for circulation as coin.

In this connection permit me to correct any misapprehension as to the purpose and effect of the Director's circular. As early as August 24, 1876, the department informed an inquirer that the trade-dollar had only a bullion value, and this information has been repeated scores of times, and published by the press throughout the country. To avoid the labor of preparing manuscript letters, the Director embodied the information in a circular, adding thereto tables for the computation of such value. There was no new decision involved in the circular, though possibly its publication may have hastened the depreciation of the coins to their true value—an event which was inevitable, and could not have been much longer delayed.

Very respectfully,

JOHN SHERMAN,
Secretary.

O. H. BOOTH, Esq.,
Mansfield, Ohio.

The third objection to monetizing the trade-dollar is that it would seriously impair the public credit, and delay, if not defeat, the important refunding operations that ought to occur two years hence, when 800 millions of United States bonds will become redeemable at the pleasure of the government. In January last, after resumption was accomplished, it became very easy to sell our 4 per cent. bonds. We sold nearly as many in the month of January as we did in two years before. I can assure you that if the public mind had been convinced that the trade-dollar was to be monetized, and that the government would adopt the single silver standard, we could not have accomplished the refunding of the 5-20s and 10-40s. The forbearance of Congress at the last session greatly aided the Treasury Department. The shadow of this fear was the only restraining motive in refunding. If by 1881 the measures proposed shall have been adopted, it will not, in my opinion, be possible to sell 4 per cent. bonds at par. But if let alone, the whole 800 millions may be funded at 4 per cent. or less. Public credit is exceedingly sensitive. Gold was the standard coin in contemplation when all the bonds were issued. To take advantage of the unforeseen fall of silver bullion to issue a silver coin worth only 85 per cent. of gold coin would excite distrust and fear. To advance public credit you must do all or more than was expected by your creditor when your securities were issued, and you get the full benefit of this in lower rates of interest and improving credit.

My general answer to your question as to the trade-dollar is that this coin ought to be left precisely where it is, a piece of silver bullion containing 420 grains of standard silver, issued for the benefit of merchants, at their cost and for their benefit, for exportation; that every one of them now in circulation is there by an evasion of the law. They were issued after they ceased to be a legal tender for any amount, and their circulation should be discouraged and refused by every citizen. If they are now monetized, it will be a discrimination of full 15 per cent. against our miners of silver who have bullion to sell, and in favor of the Chinese and of our own merchants, who, by buying up this form of silver bullion in China for 85 cents, can sell it to the government for a dollar. The proposition if adopted would suddenly change our standard of values from gold to silver, and would seriously impair our public credit and our ability to reduce the interest of the public debt.

If, however, it is deemed politic to redeem the trade-dollar and get it out of the way, the better course would be to authorize its purchase as bullion, at a slight advance over other forms of bullion, to be paid for with lawful money or by the sale of bonds. This would soon retire those in this country, without tempting their importation from China. The public would soon understand that they were not lawful money, and this would stop their circulation.

Mr. WARNER. I understood you to say, Mr. Secretary, in connection with the trade-dollar, that you regarded it as stamped bullion rather than as United States coin. The language of the law is: "The silver coins of the United States shall be a trade-dollar, a half-dollar," and so on. Is there any objection to so amending that section as to strike out the words "trade-dollar"?

Secretary SHERMAN. No. I think that the best way to dispose of the trade-dollar is to just let it alone as so much bullion, and to coin no more. I know the origin of it. It was issued simply for the convenience of merchants of California, to give them a market for their silver. It was stamped a trade-dollar, but neither that nor any other silver dollar was put in circulation in this country until three years afterward. I think its limited legal-tender quality was given it on the revision of the statutes, but afterward was taken away.

Mr. WARNER. This language that I have read is in the coinage bill of 1873.

Secretary SHERMAN. Then it was grouped with other silver coins as a legal tender for five dollars. The trade-dollar was coined at the expense of the depositor of the silver, for his benefit, and without any profit to the United States.

Mr. WARNER. Is there any longer any object in coining that piece at all for private parties?

Secretary SHERMAN. No, sir; and I should refuse to do it now if such an application were made.

Mr. WARNER. Is it not true that the owner of the bullion really gets no more for his bullion when it is divided into pieces of 420 grains each than he would get if it were divided into pieces of 412½ grains? Was there ever any gain to the owner in having it coined?

Secretary SHERMAN. Yes; there was an advantage to him from 1873 up to the time when the trade-dollar fell below the market value of gold coin.

Mr. WARNER. But could he get any more per ounce for his silver? A bar of silver containing 100 ounces will make 114 trade-dollars, or 116 standard dollars. The owner of the bar could get no more per ounce for his silver when divided into pieces of 420 grains than when divided into pieces of 412½ grains each, could he?

Secretary SHERMAN. Yes, in China he could get more. The Mexican dollar was formerly the only dollar that got a foothold in China. The Chinese would not take our old American dollar of 412½ grains, because it was less valuable than the Mexican dollar, and therefore the trade-dollar was coined, containing 420 grains, so as to make it better than the Mexican dollar, and thus win its way into circulation in China. That was the object.

Mr. DE LA MATYR. It was rather as money than as bullion.

Secretary SHERMAN. It was bullion put into a form more valuable or more acceptable to the Chinese.

Mr. WARNER. But is it not true that we got no more per ounce for our silver in the end?

Secretary SHERMAN. The government did not get any more.

Mr. WARNER. Neither did the bullion-dealer.

Secretary SHERMAN. But he got a market for his silver. They would take it in this form when they would not take it in the form of our old dollar.

Mr. WARNER. But at the time when the trade-dollar was adopted we stopped the coinage of the standard dollar. It was done in the very same act. Now, my point is this, that when our standard dollar would not pass in China and Japan at the same value as the Mexican dollar, the reason was simply because it contained a little less silver; but would it not pass for its bullion-value, the same as all coins pass for in foreign countries?

Secretary SHERMAN. No; at that time the silver dollar did not pass anywhere except for exportation to China or India. Several millions of the old standard dollars were sent to China, but they were objected to by the Chinese, and therefore the merchants of California, who wanted to make their silver bullion available, got Congress to order the coinage of this trade-dollar, which could be exported successfully.

Mr. WARNER. Then you think that by dividing 100 ounces of silver into pieces of 420 grains each the bullion-dealer did get more per ounce for his siver than he would have got for it in pieces of 412½ grains each?

Secretary SHERMAN. He did in China; he did not here. He did in China because they liked the form of the coin; just as a person is willing to pay more for one piece of calico than for another of the same material because he likes the pattern.

Mr. CLAFLIN. Did not the bullion men obtain more use for their bullion in this form than they could in the ordinary form?

Secretary SHERMAN. They did.

Mr. FISHER. They had a commodity to sell, and by getting it coined into trade-dollars they put it in a form to suit their customers.

Secretary SHERMAN. Yes.

Mr. WARNER. But it comes right back to this point, that if you divide up 100 ounces of silver into pieces of 420 grains each you get more per ounce for your silver than if it were divided into pieces of 412½ grains. Now, would that be the case in England or France?

Secretary SHERMAN. No; but we did not send them to England or France at that time.

Mr. WARNER. But when we export coin don't all foreign countries assay it and determine its value according to the quantity of metal that it actually contains?

Secretary SHERMAN. All European countries do and Japan does now; but in China they took the coin of a foreign nation and circulated it. They put a kind of stamp upon it, which did not impair its value at all, but served to naturalize it, as we might say, and then they circulated it.

Mr. WARNER. Our trade-dollar is unlike any other coin issued by any country. It has a little more value than the Japanese yen, and it has a little more value than the Mexican silver dollar.

5 SH

Secretary SHERMAN. Yes, it has a little more value than the Mexican silver dollar. I do not know that any other coin contains just the same amount of bullion. None of the trade-dollars have been issued lately, and none can be issued now.

Mr. WARNER. Then I understand that you think there is no objection to striking out the trade-dollar from our coinage?

Secretary SHERMAN. Not the slightest. I am in favor of that course. In October, 1877, I issued an order, under the authority which the law gave me, stopping the coinage of the trade-dollar. The reason was that at that time, by the gradual depreciation of silver, the gold value of the trade-dollar was less than par, and there was no demand for it for exportation.

Mr. CLAFLIN. The law gave you power to stop the coinage of the trade-dollar?

Secretary SHERMAN. The law leaves it discretionary with the Secretary of the Treasury.

Mr. CLAFLIN. So that if a demand for them should spring up, you could issue them again?

Secretary SHERMAN. Yes; the amount to be issued is left discretionary with the department.

Mr. CLAFLIN. And if a man now should ask you for trade-dollars, you would not make them unless you had evidence that he wanted to send them abroad?

Secretary SHERMAN. No; the language of the law is that they are to be coined for exportation only.

Mr. WARNER. The present language of the statute is, "The silver coins of the United States shall be a trade-dollar," &c.

Secretary SHERMAN. Yes; but the act of July 22, 1876, authorizes the Secretary to limit the coinage of the trade-dollars to such an amount as he may deem sufficient to meet the export demand for them.

Mr. WARNER. I wish to call your attention now, Mr. Secretary, to section 3511 of the Revised Statutes, which is section 1 of the bill now before this committee. The law as it now stands leaves out the word "unit," which, I believe, up to 1873, always followed both the gold and silver coins, and substitutes the words "which at the standard weight of 25.8 grains shall be the unit of value." That you understand, I suppose, as changing the standard from both metals to gold alone.

Secretary SHERMAN. I think that your insertion in this bill of the words "or unit" is substantially the same as the language of the original section. But that is a matter of criticism.

Mr. WARNER. The language now is "which at the standard weight of 25.8 grains shall be *the* unit of value.

Secretary SHERMAN. Well, I think that is substantially the same. There can be but one unit. If you mean the word unit in its singular sense you can have only one.

Mr. WARNER. But a silver dollar may be a unit as well as a gold dollar.

Secretary SHERMAN. Yes, you might make it "units," in the plural.

Mr. WARNER. But a silver dollar may be a unit as well as a gold dollar, may it not? Whether both the units are of the same value or not, is another question.

Secretary SHERMAN. That is a question which I suppose I need not discuss here.

The CHAIRMAN. Mr. Warner's idea is that this legislation, making the gold dollar the unit of value, was the turning point in our monetary system.

Mr. WARNER. Before that the standard rested upon both metals, or either, alternately, if they varied in value.

The CHAIRMAN. One was not made the unit of value to the exclusion of the other; but when this change was made silver was demonetized, and that was the turning point in our monetary system.

Secretary SHERMAN. I would suggest to Mr. Warner that he had bet-better say " a unit." But what you want to get at is my opinion as to whether we should have a single or a double standard.

Mr. WARNER. Yes, we will come to that later; but, at this point, I want to ask another question. Gold dollars, I believe, are now recoined, or it is the law that they shall be if they fall in weight more than one-half per cent. below the standard fixed by law and the limit of tolerance.

Secretary SHERMAN. Yes, the law provides for recoinage in such cases.

Mr. WARNER. What limit of tolerance would you advise for silver coins ? I will ask the Director of the Mint the same question.

Secretary SHERMAN. I have no very accurate knowledge about these technical questions ; and I think you can get that information better by asking the assayer or some of the technical officers of the mint, than you can from us.

Mr. WARNER. The States of the Latin Union make it one per cent. Should that be adopted here with reference to the silver dollar if it is proposed to coin silver dollars unlimitedly ?

Secretary SHERMAN. Our coinage is thought to be the best in the world now, because our limit of tolerance is very low, and the actual tolerance is very slight. At least that has been claimed for our coinage. But Mr. Robert Patterson, of Philadelphia, formerly superintendent of the mint, or Mr. Snowden, the present superintendent, can give you more definite information on that subject than I can.

Mr. WARNER. The most important feature of this bill is, of course, in section 3, proposing to change section 3520 of the Revised Statutes, which now reads as follows: "Any owner of silver bullion may deposit the same at any mint, to be formed into bars or into dollars of the weight of 420 grains Troy, designated in this act as trade-dollars."

Secretary SHERMAN. I suppose you would rather have me state my view as to whether or not we should have a double or single standard ?

Mr. WARNER. Yes, your view in regard to restoring silver to unlimited coinage.

Secretary SHERMAN. It would be a great object of national desire if we could restore silver and gold to free coinage ; but it is one of the most difficult and delicate financial operations that you can propose. It has been more debated than almost any other question in the whole range of financial discussion. My idea is that you cannot do it; that it is not possible to do it, and that this law would not do it, unless you make the ratio of the two metals as fixed by the law correspond as nearly as may be to the market value of the two coins.

Mr. WARNER. Do you think that practicable ? Is the market value, under the present coinage laws of Europe, so stable that it would be possible for one country alone to do that ?

Secretary SHERMAN. I will come to that in a moment. It is undoubtedly an important point. Now the attempt to make common or free coinage of the two metals, when there is a wide divergence between the legal ratio and the market ratio, has utterly failed in the past in many countries and in different ages. It is no use to try to do it. You cannot do it. The inevitable result will be that the cheaper bullion will fill all the channels of circulation, and that instead of a bi-metallic money of two metals you will have a mono-metallic money of the cheapest. That is an axiom which it is hardly worth while to discuss because it has been proved so many times.

Now let me go a step farther. If the effect of this law would be to bring silver and gold to the relative standard that you propose, it would be a great object of desire, and nobody would be more in favor of it than myself, but I am sure (expressing an opinion pretty strongly) that the only effects of its adoption would be to bring upon us the surplus silver of other nations, of Germany and of France, where there is supposed to be four hundred million of dollars of silver, and also to relieve England from her embarrassments about India; and that our gold would flow from us until we would be practically and substantially at the single silver standard upon its bullion value.

Mr. WARNER. Upon that point I would like to ask you how, under this bill, which proposes the unlimited coinage of silver, silver bullion of other countries would come here any more than it does now. Will an ounce of silver bullion, or a pound, or a ton, exchange for any more of our commodities after being coined under the provisions of this bill than now; and if not, why would it come here then any more than it does now ?

Secretary SHERMAN. Because silver being the cheaper metal, all the balances of trade will be met and all commodities bought from this country will be paid for in that coin which is the cheaper, and the result would be that gold would be as thoroughly demonetized as silver was demonetized from 1834 until 1873.

Mr. WARNER. Would that change the value of silver bullion as compared with commodities in the United States ?

Secretary SHERMAN. No, but it would reduce the value of the silver dollar as compared with our commodities.

Mr. WARNER. Then why would silver come here in the form of bullion from other countries any more after being coined than it does now?

Secretary SHERMAN. Simply because foreign nations would pay for all they bought of us in the cheaper coin, and all our values would come to be measured by the standard silver dollar, $412\frac{1}{2}$ grains of silver bullion. Now they are measured by 25.8 grains of gold, but if you adopt the double standard it means the single standard of the cheaper metal, because in the nature of things you cannot maintain two standards unless you have two equivalent values. Mr. Warner's object is all right, and I agree with him perfectly in desiring it, but I believe that any attempt to attain it by depending upon the present ratio of 16 to 1 would be as futile as the attempt of King Canute to check the ebb and flow of the sea. It is one of those operations of nature which human government cannot control. But if this government would adopt the standard or relation between the two metals which conforms as nearly as may be— you cannot come to it exactly—but as nearly as may be to the relative value of the two metals, then I believe it would be a very great object of desire, because then, if the surplus silver of the world came to us, we would get it at its market value and not at an exaggerated value. The fixed ratio resulting from this action would probably prove to be a close approximation to the market ratio for a considerable period of time. If you approximate the true relation within one or two cents, it may prove for perhaps a hundred years about the true ratio between silver and gold. In France the ratio of $15\frac{1}{2}$ to 1 adopted in 1803 was very near the market rates for a long time.

If this government is now to adopt a ratio which will fulfill these conditions, the present market values of the two metals will have to be taken as the basis.

Mr. CLAFLIN. Do you mean our government alone or the commercial nations acting together ?

Secretary SHERMAN. That is a question. Just now there is evidently a strong desire in several nations to adopt a new relation. Great Britain is threatened with great disasters from different standards in England and India. Among French statesmen there is a desire for a readjustment of this question, and I believe that if we hold firmly to our present position of a limited coinage of silver, or if we adopt the present market value of gold and silver as our ratio, we will bring the other nations to adopt that ratio. The conference that was had last summer really produced a great deal of good.

Mr. WARNER. Do you think that if we should adopt the market ratio of London to-day, there is any more probability that other nations will come to us at that ratio, or as great a probability, as there would be if we should adopt the ratio of 15½ to 1, the ratio now existing between most of the silver and gold coin of Europe ?

Secretary SHERMAN. The trouble is that the ratio of 15½ to 1 is not the true ratio between the two metals, owing to two or three causes.

Mr. WARNER. Is not the change caused mainly by the recent German and the American laws, and the suspension of silver coinage in Europe ?

Secretary SHERMAN. No; it is caused mainly by the falling off of the enormous drain of silver to India and China, by the increased production of silver, and the estimated enormous yields that are to come in a few years from the mines that are now being developed in our Western country, and also by the action of the German and the French Governments in limiting the coinage of silver. The English first commenced this in 1815; then came the action of France and other nations in the formation of the Latin Union, and then the action of the German Government, and our own coinage act in 1873.

Mr. WARNER. But is it not true that in the early part of this century the proportion of the production of silver to gold was much greater than the present proportion ?

Secretary SHERMAN. Yes, that is true; but the aggregate of exchanges as well as values have enormously changed since then. The nominal prices of things now, except in cases where human devices have cheapened commodities by facilitating their production, are two or three times as great as they were in the beginning of this century. The use of gold to settle balances of trade has enormously increased.

Mr. WARNER. To recur to the opinion which you have expressed that under free coinage we should be put at a disadvantage in our trade with other countries, or be liable to have our commodities taken from us at less value than we are getting for them now; do you really think that that would be the case ? Would our people part with more commodities for the same weight of silver under free coinage than they do now ?

Secretary SHERMAN. No; but we would be reduced to a single silver standard instead of what we have now—a single gold standard—and we would gain nothing. We are now competing successfully with foreign nations on the gold standard, but we would then be competing at the disadvantage of having an inferior metallic standard.

Mr. CLAFLIN. And would not that single standard be changing constantly in comparison with the gold standard of Europe, just as our currency has been ?

Secretary SHERMAN. Yes.

Mr. WARNER. Is it not a fact that the value of gold now, under the German law demonetizing silver and under our law of 1873 and under the laws of other States in Europe suspending the coinage of silver—is it not the fact that under these laws the value of an ounce of gold is very different from what it would have been if those laws had never been passed? And if that be true, then, by those laws (including our own law) has not the value of gold as a standard been changed?

Secretary SHERMAN. I do not think that our law has had the slightest effect in that respect. At the time the law was passed there were no silver dollars in circulation. But all the causes that I have mentioned have contributed to disturb the former relation between gold and silver. If you ask me whether that has not been injurious, and has not contributed to raise the relative price of gold, I say, frankly, yes; but how can we single-handed help it? We can only conform the law to existing facts. In adopting a new ratio we only do what has been done many times—what our ancestors did; we must weigh and adjust carefully the present relative value of the two metals. Between the time of the framing of the Constitution and the passage of the act of 1792 experiments of the most delicate character were carried on at different places for the purpose of ascertaining the real comparative value of the two metals, and when Hamilton ascertained that, he fixed the coinage ratio at precisely the market ratio. He said that it was important to maintain the two metals in circulation, but that it could be done only by adopting the market value as the legal ratio, and in this way the ratio was fixed at 15 to 1. On the same basis the French, a little later, fixed it at 15½ to 1. This divergence left the silver here and gold went abroad. We tried to correct this in 1834 by making the ratio 16 to 1, and then the silver disappeared and gold came into circulation here.

Mr. WARNER. But is it not true that what you call the market value depends very largely upon the laws of the different States establishing the ratios?

Secretary SHERMAN. It depends somewhat upon those laws, but laws must recognize facts; natural facts are never controlled by laws. Law cannot give value to a grain of sand.

Mr. WARNER. But if the laws of different countries give greater use to one metal and less to another, then do they not contribute directly to determining the relative market value of the two?

Secretary SHERMAN. If the passage of laws was the sole operating cause of the present divergence of market value from the old ratio, then the re-enactment of the old laws might restore the old ratio; but it is only one and the least of several causes, and therefore you must examine the other causes and establish your new ratio so as to get at the market value irrespective of all laws. Your laws must recognize market values, for they cannot control them.

Mr. WARNER. Suppose we should establish the market ratio to-day, and to-morrow or next month France should demonetize silver and offer her stock on the market, and call for gold to take its place in the currency of France, where would the American ratio be then?

Secretary SHERMAN. My answer to that is that I would wait in patience and expectancy until France and England ask us, as I believe they will within two years from this time, to join them in making a new ratio; or, if we are compelled to make a new ratio, it should be such a one as will not induce other nations to send to us the depreciated metal at above its market value as bullion. We are strong, but we are not strong enough to make 16 ounces of silver equal to 1 ounce of gold. The inevitable result of such an attempt would be that we would lose our gold and have a single standard of silver coin. If, on the contrary, we adopt a ratio of about 18 to 1, other nations would not bear the loss of a sale at that rate of their silver coin. The true way is to wait, using sil-

ver at the present ratio only to the extent that is demanded for convenient use, and no more.

Mr. WARNER. Under existing laws, must it not follow as a necessary
consequence that gold will still further appreciate as compared with
property and commodities generally? From the very nature of things,
must it not be so, and, consequently, will we not be subject to a con-
stant appreciation of gold under our standard if we leave it as it is?

Secretary SHERMAN. My impression is that commercial exchanges
being conducted, as they are now, very largely by paper money or public securities, there will not be any further appreciation; but that is a
matter of which you, gentlemen, can judge as well as I. Now, I wish
to say this: All our Treasury operations, which have been very heavy
during the last few months, have been conducted without the use of
gold or silver. At the end of the first fifteen days in April, after we had
paid out about $80,000,000 for called bonds, I made inquiry to ascertain
how we had paid it, and whether we had used coin, and it turned out
that no coin whatever had been used. Sixty-five millions of the amount
was paid by exchanges of bonds for bonds, and the remaining fifteen
millions by drafts which were paid through the clearing-house.

Mr. WARNER. Between countries only balances are at any time paid
in money, I believe, but nevertheless you do not mean to intimate, I
suppose, that if half of the metallic money was destroyed prices would
not be affected?

Secretary SHERMAN. No.

Mr. DE LA MATYR. Our bonds that are out we have contracted to pay
in coin, and our silver was coined at its present value. Now, do we not
appreciate the bonds when we appreciate the value of the coin in which
we agreed to pay them?

Secretary SHERMAN. Our bonds were sold at a time when the gold
unit was, as it still is, the standard of value. The silver coin has not
for nearly forty years been the standard, but, on account of the limited
amount now in circulation, has been lifted up to the gold value, in spite
of its market depreciation. It would seem to me that after we have
brought our paper, our bonds, and our silver up to the gold basis, the
better way is to adhere to it rather than to take advantage of the depreciation of silver to pay in a coin of less market value than was received for our bonds.

Mr. DE LA MATYR. You think it would be dishonest and a measure
of repudiation to do otherwise?

Secretary SHERMAN. I do not like to use the word dishonest, because
I know a great many honest men who do not think that such a measure
would be dishonest; but I am quite satisfied that it would be very bad
public policy, and that if we should adopt it we would suffer terribly in
consequence, not only in public credit but in actual loss of trade and
money.

Mr. WARNER. The Secretary has expressed the opinion here that unlimited coinage of silver would operate to expel gold from the country.
The question I want to ask is whether, under the present law requiring
the coinage of not less than two millions of silver a month, the same
effect will not be produced in a somewhat longer time, and whether to
avoid this result it will not become necessary at no distant day to change
the present law, and whether the Secretary would not recommend a
change?

Secretary SHERMAN. I do recommend a change of the present law. I
think with you that the coinage of silver dollars at the rate of two millions a month would finally (it might take three or four or five years) so

load us down with depreciated silver coin that, by the necessities of the government, it will be forced into circulation and be depreciated to its bullion value; but I take it that the good sense of Congress, enlightened as it will be by public discussion, will find some solution of this silver question. My hope is that you will suspend the coinage of the silver dollar, which now the people refuse to take, or at once return to the Treasury when issued, and await a negotiation for a new ratio; or, if that is deemed unadvisable, that it will increase the weight of the silver dollar so as to make it fairly equal in market value to the gold dollar. Then I would be willing to take the risk of the free coinage of both metals.

Mr. CLAFLIN. But as you purchase on bullion value now, the government would not suffer except by the loss of interest, unless there was still further depreciation.

Secretary SHERMAN. No.

Mr. WOOD. What would be the effect of passing this bill, in your opinion, Mr. Secretary?

Secretary SHERMAN. I think I have already answered that. I think the effect would be to bring us to the single silver standard and the expulsion of gold.

Mr. WARNER. The coinage of our silver dollar has really the same effect upon gold, has it not, that an increase of two millions a month of legal-tender notes would have?

Secretary SHERMAN. No; because we cannot get the silver dollars into circulation. We have tried it in every way, but we cannot succeed.

Mr. VANCE. Can't you pay them out for bonds?

Secretary SHERMAN. There would be no object in that. They would come right back.

Mr. WARNER. But with unlimited coinage the government would not have that question to meet at all.

Secretary SHERMAN. No.

Mr. WARNER. It would simply be with the public to say whether they would have the silver or not.

Secretary SHERMAN. O, if Congress says so, we can make the public take the silver.

Mr. WARNER. But under unlimited coinage the government would have nothing to do with putting coins into circulation?

Secretary SHERMAN. No; but there would be no gold coin at all; not a dollar.

Mr. WARNER. But that you have stated will sooner or later be the result under the present law.

Adjourned.

APPENDIX.

MONETARY CONVENTION CONCLUDED DECEMBER 23, 1865, BETWEEN FRANCE, BELGIUM, ITALY, AND SWITZERLAND. RATIFIED AT PARIS JULY 23, 1866.

[Translated by Mrs. A. J. Warner.]

His Majesty the Emperor of France, His Majesty King of Belgium, His Majesty King of Italy, and the Swiss Confederation, equally desirous of establishing a more perfect harmony in their monetary legislation to remedy the inconveniences which proceed from the diversity of standard in their silver money of account in the business transactions between the inhabitants of their respective States and for the furtherance of a uniformity of weights, measures, and coins, have determined to conclude a convention for this purpose, and have appointed commissioners, with full powers, as follows :   .

[Here follow the names of the commissioners, with their titles.]

Who, after exhibiting their respective credentials, and finding them in good and due form, concurred in the following articles :

ART. 1. France, Belgium, Italy, and Switzerland are constituted a State of Union in relation to the weight, fineness, model, and circulation of their gold and silver coins.

Nothing is changed at present in the legislation respecting debased money in any of the four States.

ART. 2. The high contracting parties agree neither to coin nor allow to be coined, with their imprint, any gold coins excepting pieces of a hundred francs, of fifty francs, of twenty francs, of ten francs, and of five francs, fixed as to weight, fineness, tolerance, and diameter as follows :

Kind of pieces.		Weight.		Fineness.		Diameter.
		Correct weight.	Tolerance of weight.	Fineness.	Tolerance of fineness.	
	Francs.	*Grammes.*	*Thousandths.*	*Thousandths.*	*Thousandths.*	*Millimetres.*
Gold..............	100	32, 258. 06	1	900	2	35
	50	16, 129. 03				28
	20	6, 451. 61	2			21
	10	3, 225. 80				19
	5	1, 612. 90	3			17

They shall receive without distinction into their public treasuries the pieces of gold coined according to the preceding conditions in either of the four States, with the right, however, to refuse those pieces where weight is reduced by wear one-half per cent. below the tolerance indicated above, or from which the imprint has disappeared.

ART. 3. The contracting governments bind themselves neither to fabricate, nor permit to be fabricated, any silver coins excepting pieces of five francs, in weight, fineness, tolerance, and diameter set out below :

Kind of piece.	Weight.		Fineness.		Diameter.
	Correct weight.	Tolerance of weight.	Fineness.	Tolerance of fineness.	
	Grammes.	*Thousandths.*	*Thousandths.*	*Thousandths.*	*Millimetres*
Silver...................... *Francs.* 5	25	3	900	2	37

They shall reciprocally receive the said pieces in their public banks under the right to exclude those of which the weight has been reduced by wear one per cent. below the tolerance indicated above, or from which the imprint has disappeared.

ART. 4. The contracting parties shall hereafter fabricate only pieces of silver of two francs, of one franc, of fifty centimes, and of twenty centimes, under the conditions of weight, of fineness, of tolerance, and diameter determined below.

Kind of pieces.		Weight.		Fineness.		Diameter
		Correct weight.	Tolerance of weight.	Fineness.	Tolerance of fineness.	
Francs.	*Centimes.*	*Grammes.*	*Thousandths.*	*Thousandths.*	*Thousandths.*	*Millimetres.*
2	00	10 00	} 5	} 835	} 3	{ 27
1	00	5 00	}			23
0	50	2 50	7			18
0	20	1 00	10			16

Those pieces must be recoined by the governments which issue them when they become reduced by wear five per cent. below the tolerance indicated above, or whenever the imprint shall have disappeared.

ART. 5. The pieces of silver of two francs, of one franc, of fifty centimes, and of twenty centimes, coined under conditions differing from those indicated in the preceding article, must be retired from circulation before January 1, 1869.

The time is extended until January 1, 1878, for the pieces of two francs and of one franc, put in circulation in Switzerland by virtue of the law of January 31, 1860.

ART. 6. The pieces of silver fabricated under the conditions of Article 4 shall be legal tender between private persons of the State which has coined them up to the sum of fifty francs for each payment.

The State that puts them into circulation shall receive them from citizens without limitation of quantity.

ART. 7. The public treasuries of each of the four countries shall receive the silver pieces coined by any of the other contracting States, conformably to Article 4, up to the amount of one hundred francs for each payment made to the said treasuries.

The Governments of Belgium, of France, and of Italy shall receive upon the same terms, until January 1, 1878, the Swiss pieces of two francs and of one franc emitted in virtue of the law of January 31, 1860, and which during the same period are similar in all respects to the pieces coined under the conditions of Article 4. The whole is subject to the provision relative to wear given in Article 4.

. ART. 8. Each of the contracting governments pledges itself to take from private parties or from the public banks of the other States the money of account of silver which has been put in circulation, and to exchange it for an equal value of legal-tender money (pieces of gold or of silver five-francs), with the condition that the sum presented for exchange shall not be less than one hundred francs.

This obligation shall continue two years after the expiration of the present treaty.

ART. 9. The high contracting parties shall put in circulation coins of silver of two francs, of one franc, of fifty centimes, and of twenty centimes, coined under the conditions given by Article 4, to the amount only of six francs for each inhabitant.

The quantity shall be determined by taking the last census made in each country and the presumed increase of population until the expiration of the present treaty.

Table for the various States.

France	239,000,000 francs.
Belgium	32,000,000 francs.
Italy	141,000,000 francs.
Switzerland	17,000,C00 francs.

There shall be deducted from the foregoing sums, which the governments have a right to coin, the sums already in circulation :

For France, in virtue of the law of May 25, 1864, in pieces of fifty centimes and twenty centimes, about sixteen millions.

For Italy, in virtue of the law of August 24, 1862, in pieces of two francs, one franc, fifty centimes, and twenty centimes, about one hundred millions.

For Switzerland, in virtue of the decree of January 31, 1860, in pieces of two francs and one franc, about ten million five hundred thousand francs.

ART. 10. The date of the coinage shall be inscribed upon the pieces of gold and silver coined hereafter in the four States.

ART. 11. The contracting governments shall communicate annually the proportion of their circulation of gold and silver, the account of redemption and recoinage of their gold and silver money, the account of the redemption and recoining of their old coins, and the whole situation, and all the administrative documents relating to money.

They shall give an impartial account of all the facts which concern the mutual circulation of their gold and silver coins.

ART. 12. The right to join the present convention is reserved for any other State which may accept the obligations and adopt the monetary system of the Union, as far as concerns their gold and silver coins.

ART. 13. The execution of the mutual obligations included in the present convention, as far as may be, is subject to the methods and regulations established by the laws of the contracting States, which are considered to promote the fulfillment, and which shall cause it to be carried into effect with the least possible delay.

ART. 14. The present convention shall remain in force until January 1, 1880.

· If one year previous to that time no notice has been given, it shall remain binding by right for a further period of fifteen years, and so continue for periods of fifteen years, except notice be given.

ART. 15. The present convention shall be confirmed and the ratification shall be exchanged at Paris within six months, or earlier, if possible.

In proof of which the respective commissioners have signed the present convention and affixed their seals.

Done and four copies made at Paris, December 23, 1865.

For France:

E. DE PARIEU.
PELOUZE.

For Belgium:

FORTAMPS.
A. KREGLINGER.

For Italy:

ARTOM.
PRATOLONGO.

For Switzerland:

KERN.
FEER HERZOG.

MANIFESTO RELATIVE TO THE COINAGE OF SILVER DURING THE YEAR 1876, IN SWITZERLAND, BELGIUM, FRANCE, ITALY, AND GREECE.

[Translated by James Gilmore for the Cincinnati Commercial.]

The undersigned, delegates of the Governments of Switzerland, of France, of Italy, and of Greece, in conference assembled, in conformity with Article 5 of the Monetary Manifesto of February 5, 1875, and regularly authorized for this purpose, have decided on the following plans, subject to the approval of their respective governments:

ARTICLE 1. The contracting governments agree, for the year 1876, neither to coin nor allow to be coined any five-franc pieces, according to conditions determined by Article 3 of the compact of December 23, 1865, excepting for an amount not exceeding the sum of 120,000,000 of francs, fixed by Article 1 of the supplementary compact of January 31, 1874.

ART. 2. The said sum of 120,000,000 francs is distributed as follows:

	Francs.
1. For Belgium	10,800,000
France	54,000,000
Italy	36,000,000
Switzerland	7,200,000

2. As to Greece, which acquiesced in the compact of December 23, 1865, by a manifesto of the 26th of September, 1868, the complement fixed for this government, in proportion to that of the other contracting powers, is fixed at the sum of 3,600,000 francs.

3. Beyond the complement fixed in the paragraph preceding, the Government of Greece is exceptionally authorized to cause to be coined and to put into circulation, on her territory, during the year 1876, a sum of 8,400,000 francs in silver pieces of five francs, said sum being intended to facilitate the withdrawal of the different coins at present circulating, and to substitute for the same five-franc pieces, according to the conditions determined by the compact of 1865.

ART. 3. Are deducted from the complements fixed in the first paragraph of the preceding article the silver coin certificates delivered up to this date, according to the conditions determined by Article 6 of the manifesto of February 5, 1875.

Is likewise deducted from the total sum of 12,000,000 of francs assigned to Greece, by paragraph 2 and 3 of the preceding article, the sum of 2,500,000 francs which the Government of Greece had been authorized to cause to be coined in 1876 as equivalent of the silver coin certificates which the other contracting governments have been allowed to issue against silver bullion.

ART. 4. A new monetary conference will be held at Paris in the month of January, 1877, between the delegates of the contracting governments.

ART. 5. Until after the meeting of the conference referred to in the preceding article, there shall be delivered no silver coin certificates for the year 1877, except for a sum not exceeding the half of the complements fixed by the paragraphs 1 and 2 of the Article 2 of the present manifesto.

ART. 6. The Article 11 of the compact of the 23d December, 1865, in regard to the exchange of correspondence touching monetary facts and documents, is completed by the following arrangement:

The contracting governments will give to each other, mutually, advice of any facts which may reach their knowledge on the subject of adulteration and counterfeiting of their gold and silver coins in the countries belonging or not belonging to the Monetary Union, especially in regard to the processes employed, prosecutions brought, and the suppressions arrived at. They will confer with each other on the measures to be taken in common in order to prevent the adulterations and counterfeits, cause the same to be suppressed in all places where they have been manufactured, and hinder the repetition of the same.

ART. 7. The present manifesto will be in force from the moment that notice thereof shall have been made, in accordance with the special laws of each one of the five governments.

In faith of which the respective delegates have signed the present manifesto, and have thereto placed the seals of their respective States.

Done and five copies made at Paris, 3d February, 1876.

For Switzerland,

KERN.
FEER-HERZOG.

For Belgium,

AD LAINCTELETTE.
BN. DE PITTEURS HIEGARTS.

For France,

DUMAS,
DE SOUBEYRAN,
CH. JAGERSCHMIDT.

For Italy,

C. BARALIS,
RESSMAN.

For Greece,

N. S. DELYANNI.

RENEWAL OF THE LATIN UNION.

By George Walker.

[From the Bankers' Magazine for January, 1879.]

The Paris Journal des Debets of November 18 contains an article, by Baron Jules de Reinach, on the new treaty which has been agreed upon by the representatives of Belgium, France, Greece, Italy, and Switzerland, by which the so-called Latin Union is continued in existence until the 1st of January, 1886. The conference held at Paris for this purpose closed its eleventh and last session on the 5th of November.

The unprecedented number of its sittings indicates that its discussions were more than usually interesting. M. de Reinach describes the conference as differing essentially from that of 1865. The latter was, in a strict sense, a monetary conference, in which no questions of principle were put forward or debated. Its sole object was to assimilate the coins of several contiguous countries, so as to give them an international circulation and a legal-tender character within the territory of the treaty-making States. The conference of 1878 was of quite another character; it was a politico-economical conference, and the president, who is also one of the presiding officers of the Paris Society of Political Economists, might well have imagined himself at one of the monthly meetings of that body.

The precise nature of these economical discussions can only be conjectured until the publication of the *procès-verbaux*, which will probably not take place till the action of the conference has been submitted to the legislatures of the several contracting states and confirmed by them. M. Léon Say has already brought a bill into the French Chambers to ratify the treaty, but the full particulars of the measure, as reported by him, have not reached us. Meanwhile the article of M. de Reinach may be looked upon as semi-official, in view of the well-known intimacy existing between him and the finance minister and the confidential position which he occupies towards the financial administration of France.

The treaty of 1865 was to expire in January, 1880, provided a year's notice to terminate it was given by one of the signatories; otherwise it was to remain in force for fifteen years longer. Rather than remain bound together for so many years by a convention, the operation of which had essentially changed since it was entered into, the contracting States would have abrogated it altogether. Switzerland, therefore, which more than any other country has been dissatisfied with the treaty since the silver agitation began, acting on her own behalf, and doubtless at the desire of all her associates, gave the notice which was necessary to terminate the union in January, 1880.

This being done, the question was whether to draw up an entirely new treaty or to amend the old one. M. Léon Say proposed the latter plan, and it was adopted. One of the most important new questions to be considered was as to the steps to be taken to wind up the treaty (*liquider la situation*) when the term of it shall have expired ; and another and more immediately pressing one was how to deal with Italy and Greece, States which are under a suspension of specie payments, and to provide against the possible contingency of other States falling into the same difficulty. The treaty of 1865 did not provide for such a state of things, inasmuch as Italy did not suspend till May, 1866, and Greece, which joined the union in 1868, was then a specie-paying country. As the case now stands, paper money has driven coin out of Italy, and the greater part, both of its full-valued silver five-franc pieces and of its divisionary token money, have taken refuge in France, Belgium, and Switzerland. For all beneficial purposes to her associates, Italy would be better out of the union than in it.

The excessive accumulation of silver coin in certain parts of the union, and particularly at the Bank of France, is an evil mainly due to the currency system of Italy. The Italian plenipotentiaries admitted this fact, and declared the determination of their government to relieve the situation by a return to specie payments at the earliest day possible. On the 7th of September, 1878, there were in circulation in Italy paper notes of the denominations of $\frac{1}{2}$, 1, and 2 francs to the amount of

112,000,000 of francs ($22,500,000), and the maximum emission of such notes authorized was 135,000,000 ($27,000,000). The total authorized issue of all denominations of paper money is fixed by royal decree of February 26, 1876, at one milliard ($200,000,000). These are denominated *consortial* notes, and are issued by the six associated banks on the deposit by the government with them of its bonds to that amount. There are, besides, bank notes not so secured, but the latter are not a legal tender.

The Italian Government having declared its willingness to suppress its notes of smaller denominations than 5 francs, the other contracting States have agreed to assist the operation by withdrawing from circulation, and refusing to take at their public treasuries, the silver divisionary coins of Italy. The arrangements for accomplishing these ends were made the subject of article 8 of the treaty, the essential provisions of which will be presently stated. By the treaty of 1865, the amount of divisionary coins permitted to each of the contracting nations was 6 francs a head of their population. By the latest census returns, this allowance gives to Belgium 33,000,000 of francs; to France and Algeria 240,000,000; to Greece 10,500,000; to Italy 170,000,000, and to Switzerland 18,000,000. Italy, however, owing to the loss of her small coins since the suspension of specie payments, has replaced them to such an extent by small notes that the aggregate sum of her divisionary money, coin and notes, now amounts to 270,000,000 of francs, or 100,000,000 in excess of her allotted quota. The whole of this excess is supposed to be in the other countries of the Union, France being understood to have about 87,000,000 and the other States 13,000,000. It will be impossible to drive these small coins back to Italy so long as the other countries continue to give them currency; and, on the other hand, Italy cannot suppress her small notes until she has coins to put in place of them. Article 8 of the treaty, therefore, makes the following provisions:

It should be premised that each of the contracting States has agreed to redeem its divisionary coins, when presented in sums of not less than 100 francs, either in gold money or in silver 5-franc pieces. This obligation is to continue for one year after the termination of the treaty. By article 8 the other States have agreed not to receive Italian divisionary coins after January 1, 1880. France is to gather up these coins and deliver them to Italy, which is to pay cash to the other States for all received from them up to 13,000,000 of francs. The French contingent of $7,000,000 is to be paid—17,000,000 in cash and the balance in three annual installments—in 1881, 1882, and 1883, with 3 per cent. interest on the deferred payments; all above 100,000,000 is to be paid for in cash. The small notes which Italy engages to retire are not to be reissued. After the resumption of specie payment in Italy her small coins will be again received by the other powers as heretofore.

Greece has coined silver *drachmas* under the treaty of 1865, and a considerable number of them now circulate in France, Belgium, and Switzerland. They have increased in those countries since legal-tender paper has taken the place of metallic money in Greece. The delegate of the Hellenic Government explained to the Conference that during the last year a loan had been contracted with the National Bank of Greece and the Ionian Bank, by which the privilege of legal tender had been conceded to their notes so long as the loan remained unpaid. The actual amount of such notes issued is 73,000,000 ($14,600,000), and the maximum authorized 78,000,000 ($15,000,000). The two banks have a specie reserve of about 16,000,000, or more than 20 per cent. Before the suspension of specie payments there were about 45,000,000 of notes in circulation, the lowest denomination being of 10 francs. The Greek Government is very anxious to resume specie payments, and will attempt to accomplish it by a credit operation, but it is not able to enter into any engagements with the other powers on the subject, nor to fix any date at which resumption can be accomplished.

The gold coins of the several States are to continue, as heretefore, of the denomination of 100, 50, 20, 10, and 5 francs, but the coinage of gold 5-franc pieces remains provisionally suspended. This suspension is owing to the too rapid abrasion of those coins. Experiments made in 1868 showed that gold 20-franc pieces used themselves up in about forty years, 10-franc pieces in twenty years, and 5 franc pieces in eight years.

Both gold and silver 5-franc pieces are to be admitted into the public treasuries of the contracting governments without distinction. The Bank of France and the National Bank of Belgium have come into this arrangement by agreement, during the full term of the treaty, to receive those coins at their counters. Although the legal tender of the larger foreign coins seems not to be explicitly imposed on individuals, they will not hesitate to ratify it in fact, as the action of their respective governments and banks leaves no motive to private persons for refusing them. Token coins (those of less than 5 francs) are declared a legal tender in payments of not more than 50 francs.

The coinage of silver 5 franc pieces is provisionally suspended, and cannot be resumed except by the unanimous consent of the contracting States. This agreement is also made applicable to the year 1879—the last year of the old treaty. An exception has, however, been made in favor of Italy, which is to be allowed to coin 20,000,000 of francs. Though not so expressed in the treaty, it is understood that this contingent is allowed to Italy to enable her to replace her old silver coins with 5-franc pieces. Even if she should elect to buy new silver of Germany for the whole amount, rather than melt down the coins of the Bourbon dynasties, no objection would probably be made, as the quantity of silver pressing upon the market would be thereby measurably reduced.

As already stated, the new treaty is to remain in force from January 1, 1880, to January 1, 1886. If, one year, prior to the latter date, no notice shall have been given to dissolve it, it is to be continued thereafter from year to year.

Although no other provisions were made in the treaty respecting legal-tender paper in circulation in Italy and Greece than those under article 8, it was nevertheless agreed to be proper to insert in the *procès verbaux* of the Conference certain declarations on that subject. Belgium, accordingly, declared that, if in future either of the States should establish the *cours forcé*, or should render the consequences of it more onerous to other States by increasing the issues of legal-tender paper, the Belgian Government would admit that the other States might take any measures proper to protect themselves. The Belgian delegate further declared that a State which should be forced to suspend specie payments should not be allowed to recover its liberty of action towards the other States of the Union, even after the treaty had expired, until it had relieved its associates from any burdens which such a state of things might have imposed on them. It is to be hoped that these cautionary declarations will never need to be acted on, and the considerable period fixed for the duration of the treaty will, in all probability, enable the States now under suspension to bring themselves into line, so that its indefinite prolongation may not be imperiled.

Baron de Reinach concludes his article, of which the foregoing is a summary, with the following passage:

"If we now cast our eyes over the labors of the Conference, we cannot but felicitate ourselves on the results arrived at, in view of the different ways in which the monetary question is looked at by the contracting States. Switzerland and Belgium do not conceal their sympathies for the single gold standard; France is bimetallic; but before pronouncing upon the propriety of continuing the coinage of silver 5-franc pieces, which is, nevertheless, reserved in the treaty, she desires to know the results of the monetary laws recently enacted in America. In this state of things it was necessary, as far as possible, to relieve the present situation, which might become embarrassing by reason of the liquidation which would have to be made at the end of the next year, when the treaty of 1865 would expire. To assist Italy, therefore, to establish her metallic circulation was not only a proof of sympathy given to that State, but it was also an act of good policy on the part of the other contracting parties. If they had precipitated matters by not renewing the treaty, Italy alone would have profited by it.

"Thus, although there was a difference of opinion between the contracting parties on the theoretical side of the monetary question, the Latin Union has been renewed and consolidated. Both governments and people will, without any doubt, learn the satisfaction that the five nations are to continue to be united by the bond of a common monetary circulation; and it is to be hoped that this union established between them in respect to money will continue to exercise a happy influence on their political and business relations."

It is not the purpose of the present article to make any lengthened comments on the new Latin treaty as it bears upon the United States. It cannot, however, be overlooked that the clause which suspends the coinage of silver for seven years longer is likely to have a most important influence on the future monetary system of this country. For the largest part of the decade which is now opening, and which is so full of promise in all its material aspects, we shall be the only silver-coining country of the civilized world. There can be little doubt that this will make us a silver country, almost as absolutely as India and China are silver countries, unless the restrictions imposed by the silver bill of last winter are rigidly adhered to—that is, a coinage limited to two millions a month, with all the resulting profit reserved to the Federal Government. This is not such a double standard as the silver party bargained for, nor is it such a bimetalism as those who favor an international system desire to secure. No party will be satisfied with it, and further legislation, either forward or backward, seems to us imperatively necessary. If we go forward, and open the mints to free coinage, all our gold will leave us, and we shall elect to become a silver country pure and simple, which is just what Mr. Goschen desires. If we go backward and repeal the silver bill, making silver token money only, with, perhaps, a large field given to it by a liberal legal-tender clause, we shall force England, Germany, and the Latin Union to face the situation, and to share with us the perils and inconveniences which a scramble for gold will certainly entail. In that scramble the United States would stand a better chance to come out unscathed than any other nation. This is the course recommended by M. Cernuschi, and we incline to think that it promises the earliest and most substantial victory to the bimetallic cause.

6 SH

www.ingramcontent.com/pod-product-compliance
Lightning Source LLC
Chambersburg PA
CBHW031454270326
41930CB00007B/992

* 9 7 8 3 3 3 7 1 6 3 3 9 6 *